AGRICULTURE ISSUES AND POLICIES

THE ANIMAL WELFARE ACT AND FARM ANIMAL RESEARCH

BACKGROUND, ISSUES, REVIEWS AND FINDINGS

Agriculture Issues and Policies

Additional books in this series can be found on Nova's website
under the Series tab.

Additional e-books in this series can be found on Nova's website
under the e-book tab.

AGRICULTURE ISSUES AND POLICIES

THE ANIMAL WELFARE ACT AND FARM ANIMAL RESEARCH

BACKGROUND, ISSUES, REVIEWS AND FINDINGS

ALBERT V. GRIFFIN
EDITOR

nova publishers
New York

Library of Congress Cataloging-in-Publication Data

ISBN: 978-1-63484-380-5

Published by Nova Science Publishers, Inc. † New York

CONTENTS

PREFACE

In 1966, Congress passed the Laboratory Animal Welfare Act (P.L. 89-54) to prevent pets from being stolen for sale to research laboratories, and to regulate the humane care and handling of dogs, cats, and other laboratory animals. The law was amended in 1970, changing the name to the Animal Welfare Act (AWA). The AWA is administered by the U.S. Department of Agriculture's Animal and Plant Health Inspection Service. Congress periodically has amended the act to strengthen enforcement, expand coverage to more animals and activities, or curtail practices viewed as cruel, among other things. A 1976 amendment added Section 26 to the AWA, making illegal several activities that contributed to animal fighting. Farm animals are not covered by the AWA. This book provides a background on the AWA and discusses selected animal welfare legislation. It also reviews farm animal research, the Meat Animal Research Center, and the Animal Welfare Action Plan.

In: The Animal Welfare Act and Farm Animal ... ISBN: 978-1-63484-380-5
Editor: Albert V. Griffin

Chapter 1

THE ANIMAL WELFARE ACT: BACKGROUND AND SELECTED ANIMAL WELFARE LEGISLATION*

Tadlock Cowan

SUMMARY

In 1966, Congress passed the Laboratory Animal Welfare Act (P.L. 89-54) to prevent pets from being stolen for sale to research laboratories, and to regulate the humane care and handling of dogs, cats, and other laboratory animals. The law was amended in 1970 (P.L. 91-579), changing the name to the Animal Welfare Act (AWA). The AWA is administered by the U.S. Department of Agriculture's Animal and Plant Health Inspection Service. Congress periodically has amended the act to strengthen enforcement, expand coverage to more animals and activities, or curtail practices viewed as cruel, among other things. A 1976 amendment added Section 26 to the AWA, making illegal several activities that contributed to animal fighting. Farm animals are not covered by the AWA.

In the 113th Congress, the Puppy Uniform Protection and Safety Act (H.R. 847/S. 395) was reintroduced and referred to the House Agriculture and Senate Agriculture, Nutrition, and Forestry Committees. The bill

* This is an edited, reformatted and augmented version of a Congressional Research Service publication RS22493, prepared for Members and Committees of Congress, dated June 12, 2013.

would require an AWA license from USDA for dog breeders who raise more than 50 dogs in a 12-month period and sell directly to the public. Also reintroduced is the Animal Fighting Spectator Prohibition Act (H.R. 366). This bill would impose criminal penalties for attendance at animal fighting exhibitions. This prohibition on attendance was also added to the 2012 Senate farm bill (§12213, S. 3240). Amendments to the Horse Protection Act (H.R. 1518) would modify the existing inspection system to detect soring and increase penalties for violations.

The Animal Fighting Spectator Prohibition Act of 2013 was also introduced in both the House (H.R. 366) and Senate (S. 666) n the 113th Congress. The bill would prohibit attendance at animal fighting events. Provisions in both the House (H.R. 1947) and Senate (S. 954) farm bills would also prohibit attendance at animal fighting events.

In the 112th Congress, two previously introduced bills were reintroduced, and several new bills were introduced. The Puppy Uniform Protection and Safety Act (H.R. 385) was reintroduced. The Pet Safety and Protection Act (H.R. 2256/S. 707) was also reintroduced and referred to the same subcommittee. The Animal Fighting Spectator Prohibition Act (S. 1947) was introduced. The Traveling Exotic Animal Protection Act (H.R. 3359) would have amended the AWA to prohibit the exhibition of an exotic or wild animal in any animal act if, during the previous 15 days, such animal was traveling in a mobile housing facility. H.Res. 736 expressed disapproval of using gas chambers to euthanize shelter animals. The Great Ape Protection and Cost Savings Act of 2011 (H.R. 1513/S. 810) was also reintroduced in the 112th Congress. The bill would have prohibited conducting invasive research on great apes (e.g., chimpanzee, bonobo, gorilla, orangutan, gibbon) and provided a retirement sanctuary for the nearly 1,000 great apes still used for research in the United States. No further action was taken on any of these bills.

In the 110th Congress, the Animal Fighting Prohibition Enforcement Act of 2007 (H.R. 137; P.L. 110-22) was enacted. The bill amended Section 26 of the AWA to strengthen provisions against animal fighting. The AWA was amended again in 2008 when provisions were included in the 2008 farm bill (P.L. 110-246). These provisions ban the importation of puppies under six months of age for resale, tighten prohibitions on dog and other animal fighting activity, and increase penalties for violation of the act.

The Animal Welfare Act (AWA; 7 U.S.C. 2131 *et seq.*) is intended to ensure the humane treatment of animals that are intended for research, bred for commercial sale, exhibited to the public, or commercially transported. Under the AWA, businesses and others with animals covered by the law must be licensed or registered, and they must adhere to minimum standards of care.

Farm animals are among those not covered by the act, which nonetheless provides a broad set of statutory protections for animals.[1]

The law was first passed in 1966 following several years of lobbying by animal welfare organizations and growing public outcry over allegations that large numbers of pets were being "dognapped" for sale to medical research laboratories. Congress amended the original law in 1970, 1976, 1985, 1990, and 2002. These amendments generally were intended to expand the scope of the AWA or to clarify various provisions. The U.S. Department of Agriculture's (USDA's) Animal and Plant Health Inspection Service (APHIS) administers the AWA. The House and Senate Agriculture Committees have exercised primary legislative jurisdiction over the act and its amendments.

In the 113th Congress, the Puppy Uniform Protection and Safety Act (H.R. 847/S. 395) was reintroduced and referred to the House Agriculture and Senate Agriculture, Nutrition, and Forestry Committees. The bill would require an AWA license from USDA of dog breeders who raise more than 50 dogs in a 12-month period and sell directly to the public. Also reintroduced is the Animal Fighting Spectator Prohibition Act (H.R. 366). This bill would impose criminal penalties for attendance at animal fighting exhibitions. This prohibition on attendance was also added to the 2012 Senate farm bill (§12213, S. 3240).

In the 112th Congress, two previously introduced bills were reintroduced, and several new bills were introduced. The Puppy Uniform Protection and Safety Act (H.R. 385) was reintroduced. The Pet Safety and Protection Act (H.R. 2256/S. 707) was also reintroduced and referred to the same subcommittee. The Animal Fighting Spectator Prohibition Act (S. 1947) was introduced. The Traveling Exotic Animal Protection Act (H.R. 3359) would have amended the AWA to prohibit the exhibition of an exotic or wild animal in any animal act if, during the previous 15 days, such animal was traveling in a mobile housing facility. H.Res. 736 expressed disapproval of using gas chambers to euthanize shelter animals. The Great Ape Protection and Cost Savings Act of 2011 (H.R. 1513/S. 810) was also reintroduced in the 112th Congress. The bill would have prohibited conducting invasive research on great apes (e.g., chimpanzee, bonobo, gorilla, orangutan, and gibbon) and provided a retirement sanctuary for the nearly 1,000 great apes still used for research in the United States. No further action was taken on any of these bills.

KEY PROVISIONS OF THE ANIMAL WELFARE ACT[2]

Animals Covered

The act applies to any live or dead dog, cat, nonhuman primate, guinea pig, hamster, rabbit, or other warm-blooded animal determined by the Secretary of Agriculture to be for research or exhibition, or used as a pet. The AWA explicitly excludes birds, rats, and mice bred for research; horses not used for research; and other farm animals used in the production of food and fiber.[3] Animals sold in retail facilities are not covered, unless they are wild or exotic animals. Cold-blooded animals like fish and reptiles also are excluded from coverage.

Businesses and Activities Covered

Generally, animal dealers and exhibitors must obtain a license, for which an annual fee is charged. APHIS does not issue a license until it inspects the facility and finds it to be in full compliance with its regulations. If a facility loses its license, it cannot continue its regulated activity. Those who conduct research, and general carriers that transport regulated animals, do not need a license but must still register with APHIS and undergo periodic inspections. Specific details follow.

Dealers, including pet and laboratory animal breeders and brokers, auction operators, and anyone who sells exotic or wild animals, or dead animals or their parts, must have an APHIS license for that activity. So-called Class A licensees are breeders who deal only in animals they breed and raise; all others are called Class B licensees. Exempt from the law and regulations are retail pet stores, those who sell pets directly to pet owners, hobby breeders, animal shelters, and boarding kennels.

Exhibitors must be licensed by APHIS as such. These so-called Class C licensees include zoos, marine mammal shows, circuses, carnivals, and promotional and educational exhibits. The law and regulations exempt agricultural shows and fairs, horse shows, rodeos, pet shows, game preserves, hunting events, and private collectors who do not exhibit, among others.

Animal transporters must be registered, including general carriers (e.g., airlines, railroads, and truckers). Businesses that contract to transport animals for compensation are considered dealers and must have licenses.

Research facilities must be registered. They include state and local government-run research institutions, drug firms, universities, diagnostic laboratories, and facilities that study marine mammals. Federal facilities, elementary and secondary schools, and agricultural research institutions are among those exempt from registration.

Animal fighting generally is prohibited by the AWA. The ban includes dogfights and bear and raccoon baiting; sponsors and exhibitors are subject to penalties. The AWA also has banned bird fights, except in the states where they are not prohibited by state law (namely Louisiana and New Mexico), and the sponsor or exhibitor was unaware that the transaction had occurred in interstate commerce.

Standards

All licensed and registered entities must comply with USDA-APHIS regulations, including recordkeeping and published standards of care. These standards deal with humane handling, shelter, space requirements, feeding, watering, sanitation, ventilation, veterinary care, and transport. (AWA regulations are at 9 C.F.R. §1.1 *et seq.*)

OVERSIGHT AND ENFORCEMENT

APHIS's Animal Care (AC) program oversees the AWA, under which approximately 12,000 facilities were licensed or registered in FY2011. For 2012, AC had an annual budget of nearly $28 million.[4]

AC officials make unannounced inspections of registered and licensed facilities to ensure compliance with all rules. Under the AWA, research facilities are to be inspected at least annually. Inspection frequency for other AWA-regulated facilities is based on risk; for example, moderate-risk facilities are to be visited about once yearly. APHIS inspectors also conduct searches to identify unlicensed or unregistered facilities. Failure to correct deficiencies can result in confiscation of animals, fines, cease-and-desist orders, or license suspensions.

In 2010, USDA's Office of the Inspector General (OIG) released an audit of AC's investigations of large-scale dog dealers (i.e., breeders and brokers) that failed to provide humane treatment for the animals under their care.[5] In a previous audit of laboratory animals, the OIG found that AC did not aggressively pursue enforcement actions against violators of AWA. The May 2010 audit determined that (1) AC's enforcement process was ineffective against dealers with repeated violations; (2) APHIS misused its guidelines to lower penalties for AWA violators; and (3) some large breeders circumvented AWA by selling animals over the Internet.[6] APHIS concurred with the OIG's findings and has implemented 13 of the 14 recommendations as of FY2013.

LEGISLATIVE HISTORY

Original Law

Although long known as the Animal Welfare Act, the original law was passed simply as P.L. 89- 544, and referred to as the "Laboratory Animal Welfare Act" of August 24, 1966. The law requires dealers in dogs and cats for research purposes to obtain a USDA license and to abide by USDA-set humane treatment requirements. It also requires a research facility to register with USDA only if it uses dogs or cats and either (1) purchases them in interstate commerce or (2) receives federal research money. The law authorizes the Secretary of Agriculture to set humane handling standards for guinea pigs, nonhuman primates, rabbits, and hamsters as well as dogs and cats—but only dealers and research facilities with dogs and cats are subject to these standards. Farmers and pet owners are among those exempted from the law. Other provisions spell out recordkeeping requirements, enforcement authorities and penalties for noncompliance.

Animal Welfare Act of 1970

P.L. 91-579 renamed the "Laboratory Animal Welfare Act" the Animal Welfare Act and expanded animal coverage to include all warm-blooded animals determined by the Secretary to be used for experimentation or exhibition, except horses not used in research and farm animals used in food and fiber research. The 1970 law also incorporated exhibitors; defined research facilities; and exempted from coverage retail pet stores, agricultural fairs, rodeos, dog and cat shows.

Animal Welfare Act Amendments of 1976

The 1976 amendments (P.L. 94-279) added Section 26 to the AWA. Section 26 is directed at animal fighting and made illegal (1) sponsoring or exhibiting an animal in an animal fighting venture; (2) interstate shipment of animals to be used in animal fighting ventures; and (3) use of U.S. mails or communication systems to advertise or promote animal fighting ventures. Section 26 contained its own definitions, authority for investigations, and penalty provisions. The 1976 amendments also clarified and expanded previous regulations covering animal transport and commerce. Hunting animals are generally exempt. The amendments passed over the objections of USDA and the U.S. Attorney General, who believed that animal fighting, was a state and local law enforcement issue.

Improved Standards for Laboratory Animals Act

These amendments were passed as Title XVII, Subtitle F, of the Food Security Act of 1985 (P.L. 99-198, the omnibus 1985 farm bill). The law directs the Secretary to set new minimum standards of care for handling, housing, feeding, water, sanitation, ventilation, and so forth. One new provision that was highly contentious at the time singles out two species by requiring standards for the exercise of dogs and the psychological well-being of primates. The law provides that research facilities must have procedures that minimize pain and stress to the animals, and describes practices considered to be painful. Each research facility must establish an Institutional Animal Care and Use Committee to review research proposals that involve animal experimentation and to provide oversight of laboratories. The amendments also increase civil and criminal penalties for AWA violations, and establish an animal welfare information center at USDA's National Agricultural Library.

Protection of Pets

Section 2503 of the Food Agriculture, Conservation, and Trade Act of 1990 (P.L. 101-624, the 1990 farm bill) extended pet protections. It required public and private animal shelters and research facilities that acquire dogs and cats to hold them for at least five days to allow time for either adoption or recovery by the original owner before they could be sold to a dealer. Dealers are prohibited from selling dogs and cats they did not breed unless they provide certified records on, among other things, the animals' origin. Other new recordkeeping requirements also were specified.

Animal Welfare Amendments to the 2002 Farm Bill

Title X, Subtitle D, of the Farm Security and Rural Investment Act of 2002 (P.L. 107-171, the omnibus 2002 farm bill) makes it a misdemeanor to ship a bird in interstate commerce for fighting purposes, or to sponsor or exhibit any bird in a fight with knowledge that any of the birds were so shipped (even fights within a state where the practice is permitted). The law also increases the maximum financial penalty for a violation (a misdemeanor) of the anti-fighting provisions of the AWA, to $15,000 from $5,000. The 2002 law also explicitly excludes from AWA coverage birds, rats, and mice bred for research purposes. The Secretary of Agriculture had previously published regulations excluding these animals from coverage, which the Animal Legal Defense Fund challenged in federal court. When USDA agreed to settle the case by essentially reversing its regulations, Congress (in P.L. 106-387, the FY2001 agriculture appropriation bill) blocked the action by prohibiting funds for such a rule change. The 2002 law made the exclusion a permanent part of the AWA.[7]

Animal Fighting Prohibition Enforcement Act of 2007

P.L. 110-22, signed into law May 3, 2007, made a violation of the animal fighting provisions of the AWA a felony punishable by up to three years in prison, under Title 18 of the *U.S. Code* (Crimes and Criminal Procedure). The law, based on companion bills (H.R. 137/S. 261), also made it a felony to trade, in interstate and foreign commerce, knives, gaffs, or other sharp objects designed for use in animal fighting, or to use the Postal Service or other "interstate instrumentality to trade in such devices, or to promote an animal fighting venture."

Proponents of various animal fighting bills had observed that in 2001, the House and Senate approved strong animal fighting sanctions in their respective farm bills, but that conferees on the final 2002 farm bill (P.L. 107-171) removed the felony language. Proponents argued that stronger deterrents were needed because animal fighting is a brutal, inhumane practice closely associated with criminal activity, endangers children where aggressive dogs are being reared, and may contribute to the spread of avian influenza in the case of live birds. Opponents countered that such measures would violate provisions in the U.S. Constitution that protect states' rights, including the Commerce Clause, and that recognize private citizens' right to travel for economic reasons. Other opponents argued that completely banning and/or stiffening penalties for all animal fighting activities would drive them further underground, undermining efforts to protect animals and the public from any disease problems created by such activities.

While animal fighting is prohibited, attendance at animal fighting exhibitions is not. The Animal Fighting Spectator Prohibition Act (H.R. 366, S. 666) was reintroduced in the 113th Congress. The bill would impose criminal penalties for attendance at animal fighting exhibitions, or for causing a minor to attend an animal fight. This prohibition on attendance was also added to both the 2013 House (H.R. 1947) and Senate (S. 954) farm bills.

2008 Farm Bill

Animal Fighting

The 2008 farm bill (P.L. 110-246) contained a number of amendments to the AWA. One section (§14207) strengthened further the definitions of, and penalties for, activities related to animal fighting. For example, the amendments increased maximum imprisonment to five years from three years. The animal fighting provision was based on language in S. 1880 and H.R. 3219 (110th Congress)—bills introduced shortly after the July 17, 2007, indictment of National Football League quarterback Michael Vick on charges related to dog fighting—to more explicitly ban various dog fighting activities, and to define the term.[8]

Puppy Imports; Penalties for AWA Violations

The 2008 farm bill also required regulations prohibiting importation for resale of dogs unless they were at least six months of age, in good health, and had all necessary vaccinations. There were exemptions for research, veterinary treatment, or imports into Hawaii from certain countries. Another section

(§14214) increased the maximum penalty for a general violation of the act from the current $2,500 to $10,000 for each violation. The regulations require that live dogs imported into the United States for resale, research, or veterinary treatment be accompanied by an import permit issued by APHIS. APHIS published its proposed rule in September 2011, and the final rule was published August 2013.

In May 2012, APHIS announced a proposed rule that would change the definition of "retail pet store" to bring more pet animals sold at retail under the protection of the AWA. Currently, retail pet stores are not required to obtain licenses under the AWA or comply with AWA regulations and standards. APHIS proposes to narrow the definition of retail pet store so that it means a place of business or residence that a buyer physically enters to observe animals prior to their sale. The regulation would exempt anyone selling animals (except wild or exotic animals) that derives no more than $500 gross income from the sale of such animals. The rule would also increase from three to four the number of breeding female dogs or cats, and/or small exotic or wild mammals, that a person may maintain on premises and be exempt from AWA licensing and inspection.

Dogs and Cats in Research

Both the House- and Senate-passed versions of the 2008 omnibus farm bill had contained the language of two other pending bills (the Pet Safety and Protection Act of 2007; H.R. 1280/S. 714) to restrict where research facilities could obtain their dogs and cats. This language was deleted by conferees; the final version instead directed USDA to review "any independent reviews by a nationally recognized panel of experts" on Class B use by researchers. Conferees said in accompanying report language that they were aware of concerns regarding use of random source animals from Class B dealers. However, they observed that USDA's FY2008 appropriation (part of the Consolidated Appropriations Act, 2008, P.L. 110-161) had requested such an independent review.

Pet Safety and Protection Act

Critics have long asserted that the limited number of Class B dealers who still collect dogs and cats from random sources, including "free to a good home" classified ads, auctions, and flea markets, are more concerned about profit than animal welfare. Others have contended that passage would leave no viable sources of random source dogs and cats, which are needed by medical and veterinary researchers because of their genetic and age diversity; and that the majority of Class B dealers are in compliance with the AWA.

A National Research Council (NRC) report on the issue published in May 2009 concluded that random source dogs and cats may be desirable and necessary for certain types of biomedical research but that "it is not necessary to acquire them through Class B dealers, as there are adequate numbers of such animals from shelters and other sources."[9] The NRC noted that of the more than 1,000 Class B dealers in the United States, at last count only 11 of them acquired and sold live dogs and cats for research and teaching. The report's conclusions and recommendations applied only to these 11 dealers that may supply such animals for research funded by the National Institutes of Health.

The report discussed in more detail the advantages and disadvantages of random source dogs and cats, which constitute less than 1% of all laboratory animals; evaluates the Class B dealer system, under which (it found) animal standards of care appear to vary greatly; and offers alternative options for obtaining random source animals. These alternatives include partnering with pet owners, veterinarians, breeders, and others; obtaining animals from Class A dealers and through donations from small breeders and hobby clubs; and acquiring animals directly from pounds and shelters, among others.[10]

The Pet Safety and Protection Act, reintroduced in the 112th Congress as Act (H.R. 2256/S. 707) would have amended the AWA to limit the sources of random source dogs and cats to a licensed dealer (under Section 3 of the AWA) who has bred and raised the animal; a publicly owned or operated pound or shelter that meets certain qualifications; someone donating the dog or cat that bred and raised the animal or owned it for not less than one year; and research facilities licensed by the Secretary of Agriculture. The bill also would have subjected violators to a fine of $1,000 per violation, over and above any other applicable penalties. The bill was referred to committee and no further action was taken.

Other Selected Bills

Puppy Uniform Protection and Safety Act

In May 2010, USDA's Office of Inspector General released a scathing report that excoriated APHIS for its lax enforcement of the AWA with respect to large dog-breeding operations ("puppy mills").[11] The report documented that over half of the kennels cited for violations between 2006 and 2008 continued to break the law. Among other shortcomings, APHIS inspectors failed to confiscate dogs at kennels that were violating the AWA, reduced punishments arbitrarily, improperly documented inspections and thereby caused nearly half of all administrative hearings involving problem breeders to be compromised because of lack of evidence. The report noted the loophole in the AWA that exempts from APHIS's inspection and licensing requirements breeders who sell dogs over the Internet or through newspaper advertisements.[12]

The Puppy Uniform Protection and Safety Act (the PUPS Act, H.R. 847/S. 395) was reintroduced in the 113th Congress and referred to the House Subcommittee on Livestock, Dairy, and Poultry. The bill would amend the AWA to bring large dog-breeding operations that sell directly to the public under AWA inspection and licensing.

The proposed legislation would require those who breed dogs to obtain an AWA license from USDA if they raise more than 50 dogs in a 12-month period and sold directly to the public. The bill also would set some minimum daily exercise requirements for dogs held by the dealers. Supporters of the bills contend that the Internet and other relatively recent marketing techniques have enabled importers and large commercial breeders, whom they call "puppy mills," to sell their animals directly to the public while evading the AWA licensing and humane handling requirements, even though they are selling large numbers of animals. (Wholesale breeders are already covered by the AWA.) Opponents, including the American Kennel Club, counter that the measures would strain USDA resources and newly subject thousands of relatively small in-home and hobby breeders, as well as rescue organizations, to burdensome licensing and regulatory requirements that were designed for large commercial businesses.

The Puppy Uniform Protection and Safety Act is similar in intent to a measure introduced in the 109th Congress, the Pet Animal Welfare Statute. The latter bill would have required commercial dog and cat breeders to obtain

AWA licenses if they sold more than six litters or more than 25 dogs or cats directly to the public each year, among other things.

In similar action, USDA/APHIS also proposes to narrow its interpretation of "retail pet stores" that are exempt from regulation under the AWA. USDA/APHIS has interpreted the AWA to include as "retail pet stores" and exclude from regulation those breeders that sell animals directly to the public. These breeders sell the animals over the Internet or through newspaper ads. In a lawsuit to challenge the USDA's interpretation, the D.C. Circuit sided with the USDA.[13]

Under the proposed change in the regulations, the AWA would now apply to breeders that do not maintain a physical place, a residence or other place, where buyers can come in to observe the animals for sale prior to purchase. This change would apply to breeders that may sell animals sight unseen through Internet, newspaper, or other ads so that the purchaser has no opportunity to observe the health of the animal prior to the sale.

It would not be difficult for most breeders to circumvent this by setting up a place where buyers can observe the animals prior to sale. In effect, the AWA regulations would still not apply to most breeders that sell animals directly to the public. Currently, the regulations only apply to breeders that sell animals through brokers or dealers.

Sense of Congress to Ban Shelter Gas Chambers

H.Res. 736 was introduced in the 112th Congress by Representative James Moran in July 2012. The resolution expresses opposition to and disapproval of the use of gases to euthanize shelter animals (e.g., carbon monoxide, carbon dioxide, nitrogen, nitrous oxide, argon). The resolution also expresses support for state laws that require euthanasia of animals by injection using sodium pentobarbital. In comparison to using gas chambers, euthanasia of shelter animals by injection is considered more reliable and more humane by the American Humane Association, the American Veterinary Medical Association, the National Animal Control Association, the Association of Shelter Veterinarians, and the American Society for the Prevention of Cruelty to Animals, and the Humane Society of the United States. In August, H.Res. 736 was referred to the House Committee on Agriculture's Subcommittee on Livestock, Dairy, and Poultry. No further action was taken on the measure.

Legislation Affecting the Use of Great Apes in Biomedical Research

The United States is the only developed country that continues large-scale confinement of chimpanzees in federal laboratories. The European Union, Japan, and New Zealand have banned or strictly limited their use. Approximately nine federal laboratories own an estimated total of 500 great apes, mostly chimpanzees, used as subjects in biomedical research. Many of the chimpanzees, however, are no longer actually used in medical research, but simply warehoused at government laboratories.[14] As laboratory techniques have advanced (e.g., computer modeling, DNA analysis, *in vitro* study) and animal research ethics have evolved, questions have arisen about the continued use of great apes as research subjects, and about the ethics and cost of housing chimpanzees.

In December 2011, the Institute of Medicine (IOM) of the National Academies published a Consensus Report on the use of chimpanzees in biomedical research.[15] While the report did not endorse a ban on chimpanzee research, the report established a set of uniform criteria for determining when, if ever, current and future research use of chimpanzees is necessary for public health issues. In January 2013, the National Institutes of Health (NIH) issued a report concluding that the 451 chimpanzees owned or supported by the NIH research facilities should be permanently retired from research and moved to sanctuaries.[16] In the most recent action to curtail research using chimpanzees, the Fish and Wildlife Service announced in June 2013 that it is issuing a new rule under the Endangered Species Act that all chimpanzees are endangered. In its announcement, Fish and Wildlife stated that a 1990 decision to declare wild chimpanzees as "endangered" and captive chimpanzees as "threatened" was flawed. In classifying all chimpanzees as endangered, the rule would prohibit buyers in the exotic animal business from taking chimpanzees across state lines, and international trade in chimpanzees would be banned.

In 2000, the Chimpanzee Health Improvement, Maintenance, and Protection Act (P.L. 106-551, the CHIMP Act) was enacted. The act created a federally funded national sanctuary system for chimpanzees retired from research and prohibited killing them as a matter of convenience to laboratories. Approximately 152 chimpanzees have been retired to the federally funded national chimpanzee sanctuary system. Approximately 500 more from U.S. research, including military, air and space research, were placed in private sanctuaries in North America. Under the CHIMP Act, however, the laboratories had complete discretion as to when a chimpanzee was considered for retirement, and under certain circumstances a retired chimpanzee could be returned to research.[17]

The Great Ape Protection Act was introduced in the 111th Congress. After referral, no further action was taken on the bill. A new great ape protection bill—the Great Ape Protection and Cost Savings Act of 2011, (H.R. 1513/S. 810)—was introduced in the 112th Congress. As was the case with the Great Ape Protection Act, the new bill would have prohibited invasive research on great apes (e.g., chimpanzee, bonobo, gorilla, orangutan, gibbon), prohibit the use of federal funds for great ape research in and outside the United States, and permanently retire all great apes owned by the federal government. The new bill would also have established a great ape sanctuary system fund in the U.S. Treasury to provide funding for the animals' retirement. Currently, Chimp Haven in Louisiana is the great ape sanctuary. The previous Great Ape Protection bill had similar provisions, but did not create the federal funding system to support the retirement of great apes owned by the federal government. The new bill was referred to the House Committee on Energy and Commerce and the Senate Committee on Environment and Public Works. In the Senate, the bill was ordered to be reported out of the Committee on Environment and Public Works with an amendment favorably. No further action was taken in the 112th Congress.

The Great Ape Conservation Reauthorization Amendments Act of 2013 was reintroduced in the 113th Congress as H.R. 1328. The bill would amend the Great Ape Conservation Act of 2000 (P.L. 106-411) and authorize appropriations through FY2018. The bill was referred to the referred to the Subcommittee on Fisheries, Wildlife, Oceans, and Insular Affairs. The Great Ape Conservation Act of 2000 supports conservation of great apes by supporting and providing financial resources for the habitat conservation programs in countries within the range of great apes. The act also supports projects of persons with demonstrated expertise in the conservation of great apes.

Horse Protection Act Amendments

The Horse Protection Act (HPA), enacted in 1970 (P.L. 91-540), prohibits the showing, sale, auction, exhibition, or transport of sored horses. Soring is a practice primarily used in the training of Tennessee Walking Horses, racking horses, and related breeds to accentuate the horse's gait. Horse soring is accomplished by several techniques, including the application of chemicals to irritate or blister a horse's forelegs, or the use of various mechanical devices.

The Animal and Plant Health Inspection Service (APHIS) of USDA is responsible for administrating the HPA and for conducting inspections at horse shows, exhibitions, and auctions. In 1976, the Horse Protection Act Amendments were enacted (P.L. 94-360) in response to APHIS's weak enforcement of the HPA. The act established what became the Designated Qualified Person (DQP) Program, an organizational structure that organizes inspections at horse events. The DQP program was implemented in 1979 (9 C.F.R. 11.7). A DQP is a person who, under the provisions of Section 4 of the HPA, is appointed and delegated authority by the management of a horse show or sale to detect horses that are sored. DQPs are USDA-accredited veterinarians with equine experience, or they are farriers, horse trainers, or other who have been formally trained and licensed by USDA-certified Horse Industry Organization (HIO).[18]

In 2010, USDA's Office of the Inspector General issued a report on enforcement of the HPA.[19] The report revealed serious shortcomings in the inspection process, with lax enforcement, repeat offenders receiving little or no sanctions, and poor documentation of inspections and sanctions. In particular, the report found that the industry's self-regulation system had not been adequate to ensure that these horses were not being abused. In the wake of this report, the Animal and Plant Health Inspection Service agreed to the analysis and put into place better efforts to enforce the regulations of the HPA.[20]

The Prevent All Soring Tactics Act of 2013 (H.R. 1518) would amend the HPA to ban "action devices" on horses, modify the existing DQP inspection system, and impose new penalties on HPA violations.[21] The "action devices," like other soring techniques, produce a more pronounced gait in a Tennessee walking horse, a racking horse, or a spotted saddle horse. The amendments apply only these breeds and apply to the sale, showing, or transportation of such horses.

H.R. 1518 would also end the horse industry's ability to self-police with industry-selected inspectors by creating a new licensing process requiring APHIS to appoint inspectors for HPAregulated activities and venues. Hiring inspectors would be the responsibility of the show, sale, or auction. The definition of "event management" would be expanded to include "sponsoring organizations" and "event managers." This expansion would make them potentially liable for HPA violations.

The bill would also increase the maximum fine for HPA violations from $3,000 to $5,000 as well as raise maximum prison sentence to three years. Trainers with three violations could get a lifetime ban from participating in shows, exhibitions, or auctions. These changes would be applicable to all horse breeds subject to HPA regulation.

Horse breeder associations have generally opposed the bill or major portions of the proposed amendments (e.g., Tennessee Walking Horse Breeders and Exhibitors Association, Tennessee Walking Show Horse Organization, Racking Horse Association of America, National Spotted Horse Breeders and Exhibitors Association). Animal welfare organizations have been active supporters of the bill (e.g., American Horse Protection Association, Humane Society of the United States, American Horse Council, and Association for the Prevention of Cruelty to Animals, Animal Welfare Institute, American Association of Equine Practitioners).

2013 Farm Bill: Animal Fighting

The AEA prohibits and provides penalties for sponsoring or exhibiting an animal in a fighting venture. Both the House (H.R. 1947) and Senate (S. 954) farm bills would amend the AWA to prohibit knowingly attending an animal fighting event. The Senate bill authorizes penalties for attendance. The House bill does not include penalty provisions.

End Notes

[1] Legislation introduced, but not passed, in the 111th Congress, the Prevention of Farm Animal Cruelty (H.R. 4733) would have restricted federal purchases of food products derived from animals to those raised free from cruelty and abuse. Numerous other federal laws seek to protect other classes of animals, often those from the wild. Examples include the Marine Mammal Protection Act, the Lacey Act as amended, and the Wild Free-Roaming Horses and Burros Act. These and the others are described, with legal citations, in CRS Report 94-731, Brief Summaries of Federal Animal Protection Statutes, by Vivian S. Chu.

[2] Unless noted, sources on the AWA are various materials provided by APHIS.

[3] For example, rabbits raised for food are exempt from AWA coverage; those for pets are not.

[4] A portion of this amount, $696,000, was used to administer the Horse Protection Act (15 U.S.C. §§1821-1831), which makes it a crime to exhibit or transport any "sore" horse, i.e., one whose feet have been injured to alter its gait. In an August 2010 petition, the Humane Society of the United States, the American Society for the Prevention of Cruelty to Animals, the American Horse Protection Association, and Friends of Sound Horses, Inc., have requested that APHIS tighten its regulations for horses by permanently barring from

competition any horse scarred from soring and requiring horse organizations to impose penalties for violations. APHIS is considering comments on the proposed changes until June 13, 2011. See Federal Register, vol. 76, no. 71: 20569, April 13, 2011.

[5] Animal and Plant Health Inspection Service Animal Care Program Inspections of Problematic Dealers, May, 2010. Report accessible at http://www.usda.gov/oig/webdocs/33002-4-SF.pdf.

[6] Large breeders that sell AWA-covered animals over the Internet are exempt from AC's inspection and licensing requirements due to a loophole in AWA. The IG report recommended that APHIS prevent large breeders from circumventing AWA requirements by seeking legislative change to exclude these breeders from the definition of "retail pet store," and require that all applicable breeders that sell through the Internet be regulated under AWA. The Puppy Uniform Protection and Safety Act (H.R. 835), reintroduced in the 112th Congress, would close the existing AWA loophole.

[7] CRS Report 94-731, Brief Summaries of Federal Animal Protection Statutes, by Vivian S. Chu.

[8] Another bill, H.R. 3327, included the provisions of H.R. 3219 and S. 1880, as well as language to enable animal humane agencies to initiate civil actions where violations are alleged.

[9] NAS, Scientific and Humane Issues in the Use of Random Source Dogs and Cats (Report in Brief), May 2009. The entire report is at http://www.nap.edu/catalog.php?record_id=12641.

[10] In light of violations noted by APHIS inspections, GAO also noted in a September 2010 report that APHIS's oversight of dealers who provide "random source" dogs and cats for research was in needed tighter managerial controls. See USDA's Oversight of Dealers of Random Source Dogs and Cats Would Benefit from Additional Management Information and Analysis. GAO-10-945, September 2010.

[11] USDA, Office of Inspector General, APHIS Animal Care Program, Inspections of Problematic Dealers. Audit Report 33002-4-SF, May 10, 2010. Report can be accessed at http://www.usda.gov/oig/webdocs/33002-4-SF.pdf.

[12] APHIS has approximately 100 inspectors responsible for over 4,600 licensed dog-breeders.

[13] See Doris Day Animal League v. Veneman, 315 F.3d 297 (D.C. Cir. 2003).

[14] The federal government began breeding chimpanzees in the 1960s for the space program. In the mid-1980s, the National Institutes of Health (NIH) stepped up its chimpanzee breeding program under the assumption that chimpanzees—humans' closest primate cousin—would be ideal laboratory models for AIDS. It turned out that apes were not as useful a model as originally believed. NIH later imposed a moratorium on its chimpanzee breeding program and began looking for solutions to deal with its "surplus." Although NIH considered euthanizing the chimpanzees, the agency abandoned the idea in favor of sending them to sanctuaries.

[15] Institute of Medicine, Board on Health Sciences Policy, Chimpanzees in Biomedical and Behavioral Research: Assessing the Necessity, December 15, 2011, http://iom.edu/Reports/2011/Chimpanzees-in-Biomedical-andBehavioral-Research-Assessing-the-Necessity.aspx.

[16] National Institutes of Health, Council of Councils Working Group on the Use of Chimpanzees in NIH-Supported Research Report, January 2013, http://dpcpsi.nih.gov/council/pdf/FNL_Report_WG_Chimpanzees.pdf.

[17] In 2007, the Chimp Haven Is Home Act amendment was enacted. The amendment prohibited returning chimpanzees to research once they were retired into federal sanctuary.

[18] An HIO is licensed by APHIS to establish a DPQ training program. An HIO wanting USDA certification must formally apply and present its proposed training program to USDA for

approval. In 2009, there were 12 HIOs with APHIS-certified DQP programs who participate with APHIS in annual DQP training seminars, clinics, and educational forums.

[19] USDA. Animal and Plant Health Inspection Service Administration of the Horse Protection Program and the Slaughter Horse Transport Program. Office of the Inspector General. Audit Report 33601-2-KC. September 2010. Report may be accessed at http://www.usda.gov/oig/webdocs/33601-02-KC.pdf.

[20] See, for example http://www.aphis.usda.gov/newsroom/2012/06/hpa_finalrule.shtml.

[21] An "action device" is a boot, collar, chain, roller, or other device that encircles or is placed upon the lower extremity of the leg of a horse. The devices rotate around the leg or slide up and down the horse's leg causing painful friction.

In: The Animal Welfare Act and Farm Animal … ISBN: 978-1-63484-380-5
Editor: Albert V. Griffin

Chapter 2

MEAT ANIMAL RESEARCH CENTER: THE ANIMAL WELFARE ACT AND FARM ANIMAL RESEARCH*

Tadlock Cowan and Joel L. Greene

SUMMARY

On January 19, 2015, the *New York Times* (NYT) published an exposé of research activities at the Roman L. Hruska U.S. Meat Animal Research Center located near Clay Center, Nebraska. The Center is a U.S. Department of Agriculture (USDA) facility overseen by USDA's Agricultural Research Service (ARS). A veterinarian, who had worked at the Center for 24 years, approached the newspaper after his concerns about animal welfare conditions apparently went unanswered by the Center. The news article described "unsanitary housing and brutal treatment of pigs; violent forced mating between bulls and cows; and hormonal experiments conducted on sheep," among other animal welfare issues.

The NYT article raised significant public concern about animal welfare standards at the Center and other federal research facilities, especially because farm animals and federal research institutions are exempt under the Animal Welfare Act, the major federal statute

* This is an edited, reformatted and augmented version of a Congressional Research Service publication R44091, prepared for Members and Committees of Congress, dated October 9, 2015.

governing animal research activities and other animal well-being conditions. In response to the article, the Secretary of Agriculture ordered USDA staff to deliver an updated Animal Welfare Strategy plan for the center and other ARS laboratories. In addition, ARS announced the appointment of the first ever Animal Welfare Ombudsman to coordinate a USDA review of animal welfare at the Center and other ARS laboratories.

The Secretary of Agriculture established an Animal Handling and Welfare Review Panel and charged it with reviewing ARS-wide research animal care and welfare policies. Following a three-day site visit to the Center in February and a public commentary period, the Panel published its final report on March 30. The Panel issued findings from its investigation of the Center and made several recommendations, including improving animal welfare training of the Center's employees and establishing clearer lines of authority in the Center's cooperative agreement with the University of Nebraska regarding oversight of animal care and use in research and teaching activities. The report also emphasized that the Federation of Animal Science Societies *Guide for the Care and Use of Agricultural Animals in Research and Teaching* (Ag Guide) should be the primary document for policies guiding animal care and well-being. While this document is cited by ARS as a guiding document in its own Directive for animal welfare, the Panel noted failures to adhere to some of the Ag Guide's standards. The most significant recommendations of the Panel concerned the inadequacy of the Institutional Animal Care and Use Committee (IACUC) at the Center. An IACUC is a requirement under the Animal Welfare Act and is responsible for oversight of research activities involving animals.

On September 28, 2015, USDA's Office of Inspector General (OIG) published its interim review of the Meat Animal Research Center. The OIG reviewed 33 statements in the original NYT article, interviewed key individuals, and conducted a performance audit of the Center. On completing its fieldwork, the OIG will issue a final report.

Bills have been introduced in Congress to address some of the issues raised by the NYT article. The Animal Welfare in Agricultural Research Endeavors Act (AWARE; H.R. 746 and S. 388) was introduced on February 5 in the House and Senate. The identical bills would amend the AWA to include under its jurisdiction farm animals being used in agricultural research at federal facilities.

On June 18, 2015, the House Appropriations Subcommittee on Agriculture, Rural Development, and Food and Drug Administration approved an FY2016 appropriations bill that prohibits obligating $56,123,000 of the total ARS appropriation until the Secretary of Agriculture certifies in writing to both the House and Senate Appropriation Committees that ARS has updated its animal care policies and that all ARS research facilities at which animal research is conducted have a fully functioning IACUC, including all appropriate and necessary record keeping.

BACKGROUND

On January 19, 2015, the *New York Times* (NYT) published an exposé of research activities at the Roman L. Hruska U.S. Meat Animal Research Center (the Center) located near Clay Center, Nebraska.[1] The Center is a U.S. Department of Agriculture (USDA) facility overseen by USDA's Agricultural Research Service (ARS).[2] The NYT article was reportedly initiated when a veterinarian, who had worked at the Center for 24 years, approached the newspaper after his concerns about animal welfare conditions apparently went unanswered by the center. The news article described "unsanitary housing and brutal treatment of pigs; violent forced mating between bulls and cows; and hormonal experiments conducted on sheep," among other animal welfare issues.

The research practices reported in the NYT article raised significant public concern about animal welfare standards at the Center. It prompted the Secretary of Agriculture on January 26 to order USDA staff to deliver an updated Animal Welfare Strategy plan for the Center and other ARS laboratories within 60 days. In addition, on January 27, ARS announced the appointment of the first ever Animal Welfare Ombudsman to coordinate USDA's review of animal welfare at the center and other ARS laboratories.

The Center was authorized by Congress in 1964 and opened in 1966. It currently houses nearly 30,000 animals and operates with approximately 117 staff. Units at the Center conduct research in animal health, environmental management, genetics and breeding, meat safety and quality, nutrition, and reproduction. The Center is operated under a cooperative agreement with the University of Nebraska-Lincoln. Other land-grant universities also have cooperative research and training arrangements with the center.

The Federal Animal Welfare Act

In the wake of the NYT article, alleged conditions at the Center raised questions about possible violations of the federal Animal Welfare Act (AWA; 7 U.S.C. 2131 et seq.). The AWA is the major federal statute governing the welfare of animals used in laboratory research.[3] Select animals used in research are subject to AWA standards and oversight by USDA's Animal and Plant Health Inspection Service (APHIS). In particular, dogs, cats, non-human primates, guinea pigs, hamsters, rabbits, and some other species come under regulation. Birds, rats, and mice bred for research; horses not used for research; and farm animals are exempt from AWA regulation.

Regulatory standards for laboratory animal welfare were strengthened in the Food Security Act of 1985 (P.L. 99-198, 1985 farm bill), which amended the AWA. It established minimum requirements for care and treatment of regulated animals in research facilities. Veterinary schools, research universities, medical schools, diagnostic laboratories, pharmaceutical firms, and other facilities that use regulated animals for research, teaching, or exhibition must register with USDA and be inspected by APHIS.

In addition to setting regulatory standards for animal welfare at research facilities, the AWA requires that research facilities using regulated animals establish an Institutional Animal Care and Use Committee (IACUC). IACUCs are composed of at least three members, one of whom is the Attending Veterinarian of the research facility and one of whom is not affiliated in any way with the facility other than as a member of the committee. The chief executive officer of the research facility appoints the IACUC members. The AWA charges the IACUC with evaluating the care, treatment, housing, and use of animals and certifying compliance with AWA standards by the research facility. The IACUC of a non-federal research facility reports compliance problems to APHIS.

However, the regulations implementing the AWA provide certain exemptions for federal research facilities. Federal agencies that conduct animal research are not required to register with USDA, nor are they inspected by APHIS. However, AWA regulations require that federal facilities establish an IACUC that reports deficiencies to the head of the federal research agency rather than to APHIS.

ARS's Humane Animal Care Policy Covers Farm Animals

Although the AWA explicitly exempts farm animals from regulation under the act, ARS's own guidelines for research practices cover all vertebrate animals, including livestock and farm animals, in all its locations under its Humane Animal Care and Use policy.[4] Animal welfare standards in this ARS policy are virtually the same as those of the AWA.

Additionally, ARS policy requires that all ARS locations using agency funds, personnel, or physical resources and engaging in research and testing on vertebrate animals establish an IACUC. ARS policy also includes oversight by an IACUC of non-ARS animals at ARS locations or at a non-ARS location using either ARS funds or personnel. The Center had established an IACUC composed of five members and chaired by the Center's Attending Veterinarian.

Semi-annual reports of the IACUC are required under ARS's animal care policy. These reports must contain a description of and the reasons for any major deviations from the requirements outlined in ARS policy. In cases of major deviations, the IACUC chair and Attending Veterinarian can immediately suspend the activity, request immediate correction of the deviation, or, ultimately, terminate the activity.

Animal Handling and Welfare Review Panel

After publication of the NYT article on the Center, the Secretary of Agriculture established an Animal Handling and Welfare Review Panel and charged it with reviewing ARS agency-wide research animal care and well-being policies.[5] The Panel established a two-phase review process. Phase 1 was a review of the Meat Animal Research Center and its activities.[6] Phase 2 charged the Panel with reviewing an additional three to five ARS locations where animal research is conducted. The Phase 2 review is currently being planned.

The Review Panel was composed of four members and an ex-officio member appointed by the Secretary of Agriculture. In its review of the Center, the Panel was charged specifically with the following responsibilities:

- A review of ARS policies and procedures for care and well-being of animals used in research;
- A field visit to the Center and inspection of areas where animals are housed or where they are involved in experimentation;
- A review of the Center's IACUC, records of its meetings, evaluation of its compliance with ARS policies and procedures used to select research topics, and evaluation of the experimental design and protocols under the IACUC;
- An assessment of the Center's animal care and well-being training for staff with responsibility for handling animals;

- Preparation of a report for the Secretary and the Under Secretary for Research, Education, and Economics that summarizes the Panel's findings; reaches conclusions regarding compliance with ARS policies and procedures; and makes specific recommendations for the Center to improve compliance with ARS standards and, where necessary, industry standards.

On March 30, 2015, the Panel published its final report on Phase 1, the review of the Center.[7] The report's findings are discussed below.

Review Panel Report Findings and Recommendations

With respect to ARS policies and procedures for care and well-being of animals, the Panel noted that ARS identified the *Guide for the Care and Use of Agricultural Animals in Research and Teaching* (Ag Guide) by the Federation of Animal Science Societies (FASS) as the primary document guiding its use of agricultural animals at ARS facilities.[8] While the ARS Directive for animal care cites the Ag Guide as a primary document, the Panel reinforced use of the Ag Guide as the guiding source for the care and use of animals at ARS facilities.

The Panel found the Center's grounds, pastures, and physical facilities were adequate and appropriate for animal care and handling, and that animal handling equipment was consistent with current industry practices. Obsolete equipment had been removed, and new animal handling facilities (e.g., new swine barns) had been designed and constructed. The Panel observed no visible signs of neglect or mistreatment of animals; animals were treated with care and professionalism, according to the Panel. The observed absence of stress among the Center's animals, their calmness at handling, and their nutritional status were noted by the Panel as "indicative of regular and high-quality animal management and care."

The Panel did note that, while handling and veterinary care were adequate to the Center's operation, the Ag Guide states that while those responsible for handling and care of animals are qualified to do so through their training and experience, the Panel saw no evidence of a "clearly defined animal handling training program with a corresponding method for documenting the completion of appropriate training" as recommended by the Ag Guide. Accordingly, the Panel recommended the development and implementation of an appropriate training and documentation program for all individuals involved with the handling and use of animals in research. As part of such training, the Panel noted that animal handlers should know how to report welfare concerns and should be knowledgeable of "whistleblower" policies. Consistent with improvements in staff training, the Panel further suggested development of means to recognize individuals with excellent animal care skills by implementing a tiered classification system for animal care technicians at the Center.

Of particular note, the Panel concluded that the Center's IACUC was not adequately fulfilling its research oversight responsibilities. The IACUC is responsible for reviewing, approving, requiring modifications, or denying proposed research activities involving animals. The IACUC was not compliant with ARS policies and procedures that call for the facility to follow Ag Guide standards. The Center's IACUC relied on a research review and consultation system that the Panel found lacked a process for formal review and approval. Nor were there regularly convened meetings of the IACUC as recommended by the Ag Guide. The Ag Guide states the various responsibilities of the IACUC regarding research protocols, objectives of research or teaching, and other activities involving the use of animals. While the Panel did not find any research projects that should not have been approved by the IACUC, the Panel concluded that the Center's IACUC was not adequately fulfilling its responsibilities, particularly its duty "to review and approve or disapprove protocols and other proposed activities related to animal care and use." Nor had the IACUC followed formal ARS procedures in approving Center research projects.

Based on these observed IACUC shortcomings, the Panel recommended that (1) the Center develop and implement processes that "promote a robustly functioning IACUC that is consistent with the Ag Guide and with current practices in the field of animal research;" (2) that no proposed research or facility inspections be conducted unless a properly constituted IACUC is in place; (3) that the Attending Veterinarian should not serve as the Center's chair of the IACUC; and (4) that the use of all vertebrate animals (e.g., rodents) should be reviewed and approved by the IACUC.

The Panel also investigated the Center's administrative and operational structure. The Center and the University of Nebraska operate under a cooperative agreement. The animal care program consists of two integrated components: (1) livestock production and (2) active research programs. The livestock production program supports the research program by providing animals that may be used in research, as well as providing animals for evaluation of livestock production management practices. Under the cooperative agreement, University of Nebraska employees operate and oversee the livestock production operations, while the Center's staff conduct and oversee the research program. The Panel noted that this cooperative agreement did not directly address oversight of animal care and welfare, particularly the specific responsibilities of the IACUC of the Center and the IACUC of the University of Nebraska.

Acknowledging what the Panel called "excellent communication" between the University of Nebraska and the Center, the Panel nonetheless noted the potential for confusion about lines of authority and oversight responsibilities. Although no incidences of deficiency in animal health or care due to uncertainty about current lines of authority were cited by the Panel, the Panel recommended that the Center develop and implement written agreements with the University of Nebraska (and any other research or teaching partners) to ensure optimum lines of responsibility for the oversight of animal care and welfare in research and teaching.

Public Response to the Review Report

An open comment period on the Panel's report was announced on March 13, 2015.[9] This announcement was followed by an open meeting of the Animal Handling and Welfare Review Panel on March 18 to discuss the draft report. Written comments were taken between March 13 and March 18. Verbal comments were taken at a March 18 public meeting. The final report included a summary of the public comments. Nearly 60,000 comments were received, including eight verbal comments made at the March 18 public meeting. Over 37,000 comments stated that all animals used in research at ARS facilities should be protected under the AWA. Over 20,000 comments stated that USDA should close the Meat Animal Research Center, require all USDA facilities funding animal research to comply with the AWA, and investigate all other USDA facilities to ensure animals were not being abused. Nearly 1,500 comments requested an Office of the Inspector General investigation and an end to the use of U.S. taxpayer funds for the Center's research.

A wide range of animal welfare organizations provided comments on the Panel's report. The Anti-Vivisection Society, while agreeing with all the recommendations, also pointed to long-standing problems with the oversight by IACUCs. The Humane Society of the United States and the American Society for the Prevention of Cruelty to Animals argued that the report did not go far enough in its investigation and ignored past abuses within other ARS facilities. The Animal Welfare Institute called for more unannounced inspections of ARS facilities by USDA. The American Veterinary Medical Association (AVMA) supported the recommendations of the Panel, especially the Panel's recommendations on the importance of training for employees handling and caring for animals. The AVMA also called for increased veterinary oversight of all medical and surgical procedures. The North American Meat Institute and the Nebraska Cattlemen supported the Panel recommendations, praised the Center's work, and emphasized the importance of ARS research to the meat industry.

USDA's Office of Inspector General Interim Report

On September 28, 2015, USDA's Office of Inspector General (OIG) published its interim review on the Center. The OIG review evaluated 33 statements in the original NYT article to make a determination of their veracity. The OIG review had no observation on 11 of the statements. On the other 22 statements, the review commented on whether evidence did or did not support the statements in the review. In general, the OIG report found that the activities discussed in the NYT article were "were generally in line with industry norms," or the review found no confirmatory evidence of the article's statements. As determined by the Review Panel's findings discussed above, the OIG review also noted that the IACUC was not adequately fulfilling its intended role. The OIG review is preliminary, and the findings are subject to change in the final report to be issued when the fieldwork is completed.

Congressional Action

Bills have been introduced in Congress to address some of the issues raised by the NYT article. The Animal Welfare in Agricultural Research Endeavors Act (AWARE; H.R. 746 and S. 388) was introduced on February 5, 2015, in the House and Senate. These identical bills would amend the AWA to end the exemption for farm animals used in agricultural research at federal facilities. Farm animal research at nonfederal facilities is not addressed. H.R. 746 was referred to the Subcommittee on Livestock and Foreign Agriculture of the House Agriculture Committee, and S. 388 was referred to the Senate Committee on Agriculture, Nutrition, and Forestry.

While H.R. 746 and S. 388 would remove the AWA exemption for farm animals and livestock in federal research facilities, some policymakers are concerned that such an amendment could be a first step to on-farm regulation of livestock at commercial farms, dairies, ranches, and feedlots under AWA permit and inspection provisions. Other observers of animal care and welfare also have suggested that including farm animals housed exclusively in research facilities under AWA jurisdiction might not be disruptive to production agriculture and potentially address some of the alleged welfare abuses raised by the NYT article. Since APHIS currently does not inspect federal research facilities, Congress could also consider bringing such federal facilities under the same USDA registration and APHIS inspection as non-federal research facilities.

On June 18, 2015, the House Appropriations Subcommittee on Agriculture, Rural Development, and Food and Drug Administration approved an FY2016 appropriations bill that prohibits obligating $56,123,000 of the ARS appropriation until the Secretary of Agriculture certifies in writing to both House and Senate Committees on Appropriation that ARS has updated its animal care policies and that all ARS research facilities at which animal research is conducted have a fully functioning IACUC, including all appropriate and necessary record keeping.

End Notes

[1] "U.S. Research Lab Lets Livestock Suffer in Quest for Profit: Animal Welfare at Risk in Experiments for Meat Industry," New York Times, January 19, 2015, http://www.nytimes.com/2015/01/20/dining/animal-welfare-at-risk-inexperiments-for-meat-industry.html.

[2] For more information on the U.S. Meat Animal Research Center, see http://www.ars.usda.gov/main/site_main.htm? modecode=30-40-05-00.

[3] CRS Report RS22493, The Animal Welfare Act: Background and Selected Animal Welfare Legislation, by Tadlock Cowan.

[4] USDA, Humane Animal Care and Use, Directive 635.1, August 1990, http://www.afm.ars.usda.gov/ppweb/pdf/635- 01.pdf.

[5] The establishment of the Panel is authorized under Section 1409(a) of the National Agricultural Research, Extension, and Teaching Policy Act of 1977, as amended (P.L. 95-113; 7 U.S.C. 3124a(e)).

[6] The Animal Handling and Welfare Review Panel did not specifically investigate the various allegations of animal abuse made in the New York Times article. USDA's Office of Inspector General is currently planning an investigation of those particular allegations.

[7] Findings and Recommendation on the Animal Care and Well-Being at the U.S. Meat Animal Research Center to the Secretary of Agriculture and the REE Under Secretary, March, 2015, http://www.ree.usda.gov/ree/news/USMARCAWHR-Panel-Report_FINAL%20FINAL.pdf.

[8] Federation of Animal Science Societies, Guide for the Care and Use of Agricultural Animals in Research and Teaching, Tenth Edition (2010), http://www.fass.org/docs/agguide3rd/Ag_Guide_3rd_ed.pdf.

[9] Federal Register, Vol. 80, No. 49, 13324, March 13, 2015.

In: The Animal Welfare Act and Farm Animal ... ISBN: 978-1-63484-380-5
Editor: Albert V. Griffin

Chapter 3

FINDINGS AND RECOMMENDATIONS ON THE ANIMAL CARE AND WELL-BEING AT THE U.S. MEAT ANIMAL RESEARCH CENTER TO THE SECRETARY OF AGRICULTURE AND THE REE UNDER SECRETARY*

Agricultural Research Service

BACKGROUND

The Agricultural Research Service (ARS) Animal Handling and Welfare Review Panel (ARS-AHWRP) was established under the authority of section 1409A(e) of the National Agricultural Research, Extension, and Teaching Policy Act, as amended (7 U.S.C. 3124a(e)), to review ARS agency-wide research animal care and well-being policies, procedures, and standards for agricultural livestock in ARS research. This review consists of two phases: Phase 1 includes an immediate review of the U.S. Meat Animal Research Center (USMARC) to be completed in 60 days; Phase 2 charges the panel with

* This is an edited, reformatted and augmented version of a report issued by the United States Department of Agriculture, March 30, 2015.

reviewing an additional 3- 5 ARS locations where livestock research is conducted. This report focuses on Phase 1 of the charge.

In regards to the United States Meat Animal Research Center (USMARC) the ARS-AHWRP was charged with the duties to:

1) Review ARS/REE/USDA Policies and Procedures (institutional P&Ps) providing requirements and guidance for care and well-being of livestock animals used in research,
2) Visit USMARC at Clay Center, Nebraska and inspect facilities, pens, fields, etc., where animals are housed or involved in experimentation,
3) Review the composition of the location's Institutional Animal Care and Use Committee (IACUC), records of its meetings, and evidence of compliance with agency P&Ps and the processes used to select topics, and evaluate experimental designs and protocols under the IACUC,
4) Assess care and well-being training needs for staff having responsibility for handling animals, and
5) Prepare a draft report for the Secretary of Agriculture (Secretary) and the REE Under Secretary (Under Secretary) that summarize the findings of the inspection visit, reaches conclusions as to whether the care and handling of animals and the capacity of facilities and staff at USMARC are in compliance with institutional P&Ps and industry standards, taking into account that ARS and USMARC has a research mission, not a production mission, and makes USMARC-specific recommendations to improve compliance, if necessary, with institutional P&Ps and industry standards.

The ARS-AHWRP is made up of 4 members and one ex-officio member appointed by the Secretary of Agriculture: Dr. Aaron Olsen, Chair (Director, Laboratory Animal Research Center; Utah State University); Dr. Lonny Dixon (Director/Attending Veterinarian, Office of Animal Resources, University of Missouri); Dr. Stephen Ford (Endowed Professor, University of Wyoming); Dr. Mo Salman (Professor and Director, Animal Population Health Institute at Colorado State University); and Dr. John Clifford, Ex-Officio Member (Chief Veterinary Officer, USDA, Animal and Plant Health Inspection Service (APHIS)).

In compliance with its charge the ARS-AHWRP members visited (USMARC) in Clay Center, Nebraska, from February 24th through February 26th, 2015. The USMARC leadership presented their duties and operation structure to the Panel during their first day of the visit. During the remainder of the visit panel members observed pens, fields, and other facilities where agricultural animals used to support the research mission of USMARC were held and handled. Panel members had free access to all areas of USMARC. The specific areas visited by panel members were determined on site at the time of the visit, and were selected by the panel members to try and view representative samples of animal handling and research activities at USMARC. The Panel also reviewed processes for research and animal welfare oversight, including ARS policies and procedures, the composition and function of the Institutional Animal Care and Use Committee (IACUC), veterinary medical care, regular review of animal facilities, and training of animal care personnel. Dr. John Clifford, Ex-Officio member, visited the site on February 19, 2015 and provided a summary of his concurrent findings in the attached trip report (Appendix A). This report represents a summary of the panel's findings and its recommendations.

Without exception, the panel observed healthy and well-cared for animals. There were *no* visible signs of poor care or neglect, such as overgrown hooves, visible injuries or wounds, or undernourished or excessively thin animals. The animals were calm and appeared used to human interaction. Indeed, all animals observed appeared to be well fed and cared for. As a rule, animals were handled with care and professionalism by dedicated staff members. No instances of animal abuse, misuse, or mistreatment were observed. Areas of the animal care program where improvements can be made centered primarily on processes and documentation associated with the role of the IACUC.

ARS Policies and Procedures

ARS Policies and Procedures number 635.1, *Humane Animal Care and Use,* identifies *The Guide for the Care and Use of Agricultural Animals in Research and Teaching* (the Ag Guide), produced by the Federation of Animal Science Societies, as the primary document guiding the use of agricultural animals at ARS sites. The Ag Guide serves as a vital reference document for the care and oversight of agricultural animals used in research for ARS. The panel, therefore, strongly supports the use of the current iteration of the Ag Guide (Third Edition, 2010) as the guiding document in regards to care and use of animals at USMARC.

USMARC ADMINISTRATIVE AND OPERATIONAL STRUCTURE

Finding 1

There is a lack of clarity on specific lines of authority and responsibility for oversight in regards to animal care and welfare in the cooperative arrangement between USMARC and the University of Nebraska-Lincoln.

The USMARC functions as a unique experimental facility in its ability to evaluate many aspects of livestock production in a manner consistent with current livestock industry practices. To achieve this the facility performs multiple essential supporting operations such as crop production, animal feed storage and preparation, and pasture management.

Administratively, the USMARC is operated in close cooperation with the University of Nebraska- Lincoln (UNL) under a specific cooperative agreement, by which UNL employees provide services for all aspects of facility maintenance and operation while USMARC employees are directly involved in the administration and conduct of research activities. The cooperative agreement does not directly mention oversight of animal care and welfare particularly the responsibilities of IACUCs from USMARC and UNL.

The animal care program consists of two distinct, but closely integrated components: livestock production and active research programs. The livestock production operation supports the research endeavor of the center by providing animals that may be used in research projects and by providing production systems for evaluating aspects of livestock production management, such as construction and orientation of beef cattle feedlots and improved pasture management. Under the specific cooperative agreement UNL employees operate and oversee the livestock production operations while USMARC employees conduct and oversee the research programs, although effective management requires close coordination and communication between UNL and USMARC staff.

Veterinary care is also provided via a cooperative process. The USMARC employs a full-time veterinarian who acts as the attending veterinarian, participates as chair of the IACUC, and is responsible for the direction of veterinary care at USMARC. The Attending Veterinarian receives expanded support for clinical care from the Great Plains Veterinary Education Center (GPVEC), a component of the School of Veterinary Medicine at UNL. The GPVEC uses experienced and licensed veterinarians working with veterinary students from various US veterinary colleges, who are completing the clinical years of their professional degree, to examine and treat illness and injury to USMARC animals. In this manner USMARC and GPVEC provide an important learning opportunity to the next generation of food animal veterinarians in recognizing and responding to animal health needs in a livestock production environment.

It is the opinion of the panel members that there is strong administrative support for the animal care program. This was evidenced by the strong and constant communication between the Center Director, the USMARC veterinarian, and the UNL animal care staff. Further evidence of the administrative commitment to the animal care program was the strong involvement of the Center Director and other members of the center administrative team in the panel review process.

There appears to be excellent communication between the multiple parties involved in animal care, veterinary care, and animal research. There is, however, the potential for confusion about lines of authority and oversight responsibility. Procedures for animal care and use are also not adequately documented. Clear lines of authority are particularly vital in areas of animal health, well-being and veterinary care. The panel did not identify specific instances of deficiency in animal health or veterinary care due to uncertainty about lines of authority. But the development and implementation of written agreements between USMARC and UNL which define responsibilities and authority for all aspects of animal care can improve clarity for all parties involved and can assist in ensuring appropriate animal care. Topics for consideration to be included in written agreements include: research oversight (via Institutional Animal Care and Use Committees), financial responsibilities, oversight and maintenance of physical facilities, and authority and responsibility to provide veterinary medical care in cases of animal illness or injury.

Recommendation 1

USMARC should develop and implement written agreements with UNL and any other research or teaching partners to ensure optimum lines of responsibility for the oversight of animal care and use in research and teaching activities.

Physical Facilities and Equipment

The USMARC is an approximately 33,000 acre research site. The site houses swine, sheep, and beef cattle. The site includes numerous pasture areas and crop fields. Also on site are located administrative and research buildings, a USDA inspected abattoir, facilities for the GPVEC, and multiple animal barns and associated structures distributed throughout the research site grounds. The panel had free access to any structure or location at the research site, and observed representative examples of animal working and holding areas.

It is the opinion of the panel that the grounds, pastures, and physical facilities are adequate and appropriate to the intended purpose of animal handling and care, and in some instances the facilities are excellent. Animal handling equipment throughout the facility was found to be consistent with current practices in the animal production industry. In the beef cattle areas the animal handling gates, alleys, and chutes have been specifically designed to minimize animal stress during routine animal movement and handling. The swine facilities are consistent with best industry practices including "shower-in and shower out" capabilities. Swine pens are appropriately sized and consistent with the space recommendations in the Ag Guide (Table 11-2) including appropriate ventilation, adequate space, and high level of biosecurity. Sheep facilities contain appropriate equipment and areas for housing and caring for newborn sheep and their dams, and appropriate facilities for the care of orphaned animals as well.

There is also evidence of strong administrative support for appropriate animal handling facilities. The USMARC has been removing obsolete animal handling structures while also committing significant resources to the construction of new animal handling facilities, in particular the construction of new swine barns to both replace and supplement current swine housing facilities. As appropriate the USMARC has sought outside consultation on design and construction of new facilities to supplement on-site expertise.

ANIMAL HANDLING AND VETERINARY CARE

Finding 2

At this time there is no evidence for a clearly defined animal handling training program with a corresponding method for documenting the completion of appropriate training.

As part of the panel site visit panel members observed several instances of animal handling by UNL and USMARC staff. Observations were made at the beef cattle feedlot, at beef cattle pasture areas, within the sheep area, within swine facilities, and at the abattoir. Panel members also interviewed the USMARC Attending Veterinarian, the director of the GPVEC, and members of the UNL animal care staff to understand and evaluate the animal handling and care program and the veterinary care program for USMARC animals.

Among all animals observed the panel found no visible signs of neglect or mistreatment. There were no visible signs of poor care or neglect, such as overgrown hooves, visible injuries or wounds, or undernourished or excessively thin animals. The animals were calm and appeared used to human interaction. Indeed, all animals observed appeared to be well fed and cared for. We find these observations to be a good indication of how animals are routinely cared for at USMARC. This may be particularly significant as the Panel visited USMARC towards the end of the winter season. It is not uncommon for livestock in general, and pasture fed animals in particular, to have the potential to lose body weight during winter months due to decreased forage and increased metabolic energy demands associated with cold environments. We believe that to observe well-nourished animals at this time of year is indicative of regular and ongoing high quality animal management and care.

In all instances where panel members directly observed animal handling it was noted that animals were treated with care and professionalism. Animals were observed to be calm, without any obvious signs of stress such as excessive vocalization, visually apparent agitation, or attempts to escape holding pens or chutes. We find these observations of animal behavior during handling to be significant as we believe it is indicative of how animals are routinely handled at the facility and not just during the week of the Panel's visit.

The training of animal care staff appeared to be adequate and appropriate, as demonstrated by the skills observed during animal handling. The panel was also provided with examples where individual technicians demonstrated exceptional animal handling skills. Furthermore, the USMARC has established a three-tiered classification system for its technicians to recognize and promote individuals who display strong animal handling skills within the beef cattle unit. Therefore, no deficiencies or concerns regarding the humane handling and care of livestock were observed, and many of the animal care practices are to be commended.

The veterinary medical care program is appropriate to the operation. The USMARC Attending Veterinarian has guided the development of routine animal care standard operation procedures (SOPs) and has developed detailed SOPs to guide veterinary medical care within the various species care teams. The facility has also developed a high quality in-house electronic medical records database for tracking the health and medical care for all swine and beef cattle. The medical database is available to all animal care and veterinary staff and assists in communicating the health and well-being of individual animals as well as animal groups across the entire animal care program at the USMARC. There is also evidence of strong cooperation between the USMARC veterinarian and GPVEC veterinary staff with consultation between the units in response to disease outbreaks and routine veterinary care. The electronic medical records database has not yet been implemented for sheep. Extending this capability to cover the sheep research and production programs will assist in tracking overall flock health and help in identifying potential areas for concern. Efforts to expand the database capabilities to cover sheep should be encouraged.

While the panel found animal handling and veterinary care programs to be adequate to the operation, with specific examples of excellent animal care, there are areas where improvements can be made. The Ag Guide states "It is the responsibility of the institution to ensure that scientists, agricultural animal care staff, students, and other individuals who care for or use agricultural animals are qualified to do so through training or experience." At this time there is no evidence for a clearly defined animal handling training program with a corresponding method for documenting the completion of appropriate training. The Ag Guide further states "Training programs should be tailored to institutional animal user needs but provide information about the humane care and use of agricultural animals, including, if applicable, 1) husbandry needs, proper handling, surgical procedures, and pre- and post-procedural care; 2) methods for minimizing the number of animals used and techniques for minimizing pain and distress, including the proper use of anesthetics, analgesics, tranquilizers, and non-pharmacologic methods; 3) methods for reporting deficiencies in the animal care program; 4) use of information services such as the Animal Welfare Information

Center at the National Agricultural Library (NRC, 1991; CFR, 1992); and 5) methods of euthanasia. Records of participation in training programs should be maintained and available for review as needed."

Recommendation 2

USMARC should develop and implement an appropriate training and documentation program for all individuals involved with the handling and use of animals in research. An explicit component of this training should be clear directions on how to report concerns regarding animal welfare. Various available national training components can be used for this purpose. As an important component of training on how to report welfare concerns, individuals should be informed of "whistleblower" policies which protect individuals who choose to report concerns. Copies of the whistleblower policy and contact information for reporting animal welfare concerns should be clearly posted in all animal handling areas.

Recommendation 3

USMARC should extend the electronic medical records database to include all species housed at USMARC. This will assist in monitoring both individual and herd health of all animals, and provide assurance that animals are receiving the appropriate care.

While it is expected that all individuals at USMARC involved in animal care or research (scientists, technicians, animal caretakers, etc.) will participate in the training program it is expected that training will be tailored to the specific needs of USMARC and UNL, and tailored to the work responsibilities of individuals. The panel notes that in addition to on-the job training and directed on-site training there are multiple existing resources that may be considered for inclusion in the training program, such as the Collaborative Institutional Training Initiative (CITI), the Learning Library from the American Association for Laboratory Animal Science (AALAS) and Ag Learn from the USDA. The University of Nebraska-Lincoln has an established animal care program, and may also be an appropriate resource to consider while developing the training program.

In addition to the development of a well-defined training program the panel suggests that means be developed to recognize individuals with excellent animal care skills across all areas of USMARC by implementing a tiered classification system for animal care technicians comparable to that already in place for beef cattle animal care staff. The panel also suggests that efforts be made to disseminate best practices or innovative methods for improving animal handling and care within ARS and to the livestock industry in general. This may be done by developing means for sharing practices within USMARC and between existing ARS units. This may also be accomplished by encouraging individuals associated with animal care to present their innovative animal handling techniques in a variety of forums such as producers meetings, regional and national scientific conferences, and in trade and peer-reviewed publications.

SELECTION OF RESEARCH TOPICS AND RESEARCH OVERSIGHT BY THE INSTITUTIONAL ANIMAL CARE AND USE COMMITTEE

Finding 3

The Institutional Animal Care and Use Committee at USMARC was not adequately fulfilling its intended role of providing research oversight by reviewing and approving, requiring modifications in or denying proposed research activities. This is not compliant with ARS Policies and Procedures that call for facilities to follow the standards outlined in the Ag Guide.

ARS research is organized into National Programs. These programs are designed to bring coordination and communication across multiple research sites and projects operated by ARS. The National Programs focus on the relevance, impact, and quality of ARS Research. ARS makes extensive efforts to communicate with stakeholders on pressing needs in the animal production industry. This communication helps guide the development of National Programs for ARS research. These National Programs in turn are used as criteria for evaluating proposed research projects at ARS sites. National Programs that provide overall guidance at USMARC include Food Animal Production (NP 101), Animal Health (NP 103), Food Safety (NP 108), and Agricultural and Industrial Byproducts (NP 214). All research projects using animals at USMARC have been evaluated and reviewed by the Center Director for their merit and significance as it aligns with one or more of these National Programs.

The USMARC has an 8 member Institutional Animal Care and Use Committee (IACUC) consisting of the USMARC veterinarian, who acts as committee chair, and other USMARC employees (scientists, animal care technicians and a veterinary technician). Until immediately prior to the panel site inspection an appropriate unaffiliated member was also present. The development of a conflict of interest due to the employment status of an immediate family member required this individual to conclude his term of service on the IACUC.

Based upon interviews with the Center Director, the management team and the USMARC Attending Veterinarian the following process for reviewing and approving research projects was described: The first step consisted of an informal process involving the research scientist proposing a study, the Center Director, the Attending Veterinarian, and any animal unit managers who may be involved by providing animals or other resources. The informal review process provided a valuable vetting process to identify and address concerns about animal welfare, experimental design, and resource allocation. Following discussions and input from the various parties a description of the proposed research was captured in an Experimental Outline (EO) document. The EO was then circulated for review and final approval by the Center Director, Attending Veterinarian, and any animal unit or facility managers who would be involved in conducting the project. The EO was then provided to IACUC for review and comment. However, there was no evidence of formal review or approval of the proposed research by IACUC members. Furthermore, there was no evidence of regular convened meetings of the IACUC, as recommended by the Ag Guide.

The IACUC members did conduct semi-annual inspections of animal handling areas and facilities, helping to identify issues with physical facilities that would require correction. Written reports summarizing these inspections were provided to the Center Director. In December 2014, the Chair of the IACUC implemented improvements to the process for reviewing the experimental outlines. All EOs were emailed to the IACUC members for review. If there were any concerns, the Chair convened a meeting of the IACUC to discuss.

In regards to the responsibilities of the IACUC the Ag Guide states: "The IACUC is authorized to:

- review and approve or disapprove protocols and other proposed activities, or proposed significant changes in activities, related to agricultural animal care and use in research and teaching;

- conduct, at least twice a year, an inspection of agricultural animal facilities and study areas and review of the overall agricultural animal care and use program, and to provide a written report to the responsible institutional official regarding the institution's compliance with this guide;
- investigate concerns, complaints, or reports of noncompliance involving agricultural animals at the facility;
- suspend an activity involving agricultural animals when it is not in compliance with approved protocols or written operating procedures;
- make recommendations regarding the development and implementation of institutional policies and procedures to facilitate, support, and monitor the humane and appropriate use of animals in agricultural research and teaching as well as any other aspect of the agricultural animal care program; and
- perform other functions as may be required by institutional need and by applicable laws, regulations, and policies."

The review of research and teaching activities by an IACUC, with the subsequent approval, request for modifications or denial of the proposed activities, is one of the most important functions of the IACUC. The Ag Guide recommends that when reviewing proposed animal use the following topics should be considered:

- Objectives and significance of the research or teaching activity;
- Avoiding unnecessary duplication of previous studies;
- Availability or appropriateness of alternative procedures or models (e.g., less invasive procedures, cell or tissue culture, or computer simulations) for the proposed research or teaching activity. It should be noted, however, that hands-on training involving animals is a particularly important component of agricultural research and teaching;
- Aspects of the proposed experiment or demonstration having to do directly with animal care and use, including justification for the species and (or) strain of animal used; justification for the number of animals used; and a description of procedures that may cause discomfort, distress, or pain and of methods of alleviation including anesthesia, analgesia, tranquilizers, and nonpharmacologic means,

as well as justification for any procedures that involve unalleviated pain, discomfort, or distress;

- Appropriateness of procedures and post-procedural care;
- Criteria and process for timely intervention, removal of animals from a study, or euthanasia if painful and stressful outcomes are anticipated;
- Unusual husbandry requirements;
- Aspects of animal husbandry not covered under written operating procedures;
- Method of euthanasia or disposition of the animal; and
- Responsibilities, training, and qualifications of the researchers, teachers, students, and animal care personnel involved in the proposed activities.

Based upon the findings of the panel, the USMARC IACUC was not adequately fulfilling its responsibilities, particularly in regards to its duty to "review and approve or disapprove protocols and other proposed activities, or proposed significant changes in activities, related to agricultural animal care and use in research and teaching."

For the IACUC to perform its function as intended committee members must be fully informed and knowledgeable about their duties and expectations. To assist the IACUC in fulfilling its duty, committee members should receive additional training on the appropriate functioning of an IACUC. The panel does not intend to prescribe the exact mechanism for obtaining this training, but notes that organizations such as Public Responsibility in Medicine and Research (PRIM&R) have produced seminars and other training information which has been widely used by academia and biomedical research institutions to assist in establishing best practices for research oversight. The University of Nebraska-Lincoln is a regional resource that includes individuals experienced in animal research oversight. The close working relationship between UNL and USMARC can provide opportunities to receive guidance on principles of research oversight.

It is also important to provide training to all individuals associated with animal care or research receive training on the role and importance of the IACUC in animal welfare and oversight. The training may be incorporated into the overall training program as recommended above. On-line training courses and other materials are available that can be recommended to be used by USMARC.

The informal review by Center management and veterinary care members is a valuable tool that can quickly identify and correct or prevent experiments that may have deficiencies in experimental design or animal welfare. Further, the experimental outline document contained some components that should be reviewed by an IACUC. However, other review processes, whether informal or formal, cannot replace the oversight review by an IACUC. USMARC should develop a consistent IACUC review process that will review and evaluate the topics related to animal welfare as indicated by the Ag Guide. While not required, many institutions develop standardized research proposal forms and written IACUC standard operating practices that assist committee members and scientists in developing and reviewing research proposals to ensure appropriate animal welfare. The development of such standardized written procedures and forms may assist the USMARC IACUC in appropriately fulfilling its stated purpose.

The Ag Guide indicates the IACUC should meet at regular intervals, and at least once every six months, to ensure that the use of animals in research is humane, appropriate, and in accordance with the Ag Guide. The meeting must be held with a quorum of members present, actions of the committee should be conducted by vote of a majority of the quorum present, and committee actions should be recorded in meeting minutes. Although review and approval of research proposals may be appropriately conducted outside of convened committee meetings, discussion of research activities generally results in additional scrutiny and may help identify appropriate safeguards to animal welfare, including identifying criteria for veterinary medical intervention and/or animal euthanasia in animal research projects. As there is currently no evidence that such meetings have occurred with any regularity, compliance with the standards of the Ag Guide will require that properly convened meetings be held at regular intervals, and that criteria be developed for what types of research proposals should receive additional review and discussion at IACUC meetings and those that may be appropriately reviewed by designated IACUC members outside of a convened meeting.

In accordance with the Ag Guide an IACUC should consist of no fewer than five members and should be composed of individuals who are qualified by experience or training to evaluate the programs and proposals under review. The committee should include at least one individual from each of the following categories:

- A scientist who has experience in agricultural research or teaching involving agricultural animals;

- An animal, dairy, or poultry scientist who has training and experience in the management of agricultural animals;
- A veterinarian who has training and experience in agricultural animal medicine and who is licensed or eligible to be licensed to practice veterinary medicine;
- A person whose primary concerns are in an area outside of science
- A person who is not affiliated with the institution and who is not a family member of an individual affiliated with the institution. This public member is intended to provide representation for general community interests in the proper care and treatment of animals and should not be a person who uses animals in agricultural or biomedical research or teaching activities at the college or university level; and
- Other members as required by institutional needs and applicable laws, regulations, and policies.

Individuals with appropriate experience and training may fulfill more than a single role on the IACUC. The panel recognizes that the IACUC was properly constituted until the recent, and appropriate, recusal of the non-affiliated member due to potential conflict of interest. However, no formal IACUC review functions should be performed until an appropriate replacement is found. Furthermore, if at any time in the future a properly constituted IACUC is not present at USMARC all research review functions should be suspended until an appropriate committee is reconstituted.

The panel also noted that the USMARC Attending Veterinarian is serving as the IACUC chair. While this arrangement is not prohibited by the Ag Guide or any animal oversight regulations such an arrangement is generally considered to be less than ideal. Situations where the attending veterinarian also serves as the chair sometimes encourages other committee members to not be fully engaged in the review process, assuming the veterinarian will provide adequate oversight. It also has the potential to set up a conflict of interest as veterinarians hold a vital role as advocates for animal welfare. Ideally the IACUC chair will be a senior individual within the institution with the respect of peers and with a strong commitment to animal welfare.

While present, panel members were informed that a small number of research mice are also housed at the facility. While a very minor component of the overall animal research program at USMARC it is best practice that all vertebrate animals used in research receive appropriate oversight protections by the IACUC. When using species other than livestock as research models the IACUC should use the appropriate guiding documents instead of the Ag

Guide. In the case of mice, the *Guide for the Care and Use of Laboratory Animals* (Eighth Edition, 2011) is considered the gold-standard of laboratory animal care.

Recommendation 4

USMARC should develop and implement processes that promote a robustly functioning IACUC that is consistent with the Ag Guide and with current practices in the field of animal research. Important components of complying with this recommendation include:

- Appropriate training for IACUC members on processes, requirements, and expectations.
- Properly convened meetings be held regularly, and that criteria be developed for what types of research proposals should receive additional review and discussion at IACUC meetings and those that may be appropriately reviewed by designated IACUC members outside of a convened meeting
- Development of a consistent IACUC review process that will review and evaluate the topics related to animal welfare as indicated by the Ag Guide.
- All individuals associated with animal care or research receive training on the role and importance of the IACUC in animal welfare and oversight.
- IACUC members should inspect all areas where animals are held, handled or used, even if animals are not present at the time of inspection.

Recommendation 5

No reviews of proposed research or facility inspections be conducted unless a properly constituted IACUC is in place.

Recommendation 6

The Panel suggests that the Attending Veterinarian should not serve as the chair of the USMARC IACUC.

Recommendation 7

Use of all vertebrate animals at USMARC should be reviewed and approved by the IACUC. This includes animals used solely for production and any non-livestock animals such as rodents.

CONCLUSION

The Agricultural Research Service - Animal Handling and Welfare Panel visited the United States Meat Animal Research Center in Clay Center, Nebraska, to evaluate its animal care and use program. Based upon the observations of the panel members *no evidence* of poor animal handling, animal abuse, or inadequate veterinary care was observed or identified. However, the facility was found to not be in full compliance with ARS policies and procedures in that the facility did not fully comply with the intent or guidance within the Guide for the Care and Use of Agricultural Animal is Research and Teaching, particularly in regards to the conduct and documentation of animal handling training programs and the conduct of the Institutional Animal Care and Use Committee. The panel has provided recommendations specific to assist the Center to become compliant with ARS policies and procedures and with best practices in the field of animal research.

APPENDIX A. DR. JOHN CLIFFORD'S TRIP REPORT

From:	Christensen laura C - APHIS on behalf of Clifford. John R - APHIS
To:	Esch Michele
Subject:	Clifford Trip Report
Date:	Friday, February 27, 2015 10:21:02 AM

Clifford Trip Report

On February 19, 2015 I met with members of ARS and UNL at the USMARC facility in Clay Center, Nebraska. The day started with an overview of the entire campus that included the number of acres, animals and personnel at the facility. It also included the relationship between UNL and ARS. They went through a number of topics that included research projects and the topics that were raised in the New York Times article. They also explained how research projects were approved.

I then toured the facilities and observed a number of the livestock. It included cattle and sheep. I did not go into the swine facilities due to my limited time. The swine facility is a shower in and shower out facility. I also did not go into the necropsy areas.

In the afternoon I met with more of the staff for general discussion. Observations:

The staff was very helpful and professional. They provided a great deal of material for my review. They offered to take me to any part of the facility. The animals that I saw were well cared for and in good body condition. Employees appear to have a very caring attitude of their work and care of the animals_

Recommendations:

There appears to be a formal and informal process for research project approvals. There needs to be one process that is followed. There also needs to be notes taken of the discussions that indicate any concerns raised and include approval or disapproval of any project. I believe they do take personal interest and care of animals but need to keep better records of formal process_

There is a health database that is used for the cattle and swine. There are plans to expand to the sheep. I would make this a priority and speed up that process.

Laura C. Christensen
Chief of Staff APHIS-VS

Appendix B – Summary of Public Comment

The open comment period was held between March 9, 2015, and March 18, 2015. Written comments were submitted to a specific email box or the REE Advisory Board Office. A total of 59,660 written comments were received during this time frame. At the public meeting on March 18, 2015, 8 verbal comments were received. Below is a summary of the public comments received:

Written Comments

37,389 comments	Secretary Vilsack should immediately require that all animals used in research at
	USMARC and other USDA facilities be protected under the Animal Welfare Act standards. The USDA should also appoint outside experts in order to assure that all recommendations are properly implemented.
20,678 comments	The USDA must: Shut down all research at the USMARC facility; Require all USDA funded agricultural animal research to comply with the Animal Welfare Act
	(AWA), including the AWA requirements for reporting and transparency;
	Conduct a thorough investigation to ensure that similar animal welfare abuses are not occurring at other USDA research facilities or as a part of any USDA-funded research conducted elsewhere.
1,474 comments	Requested an unbiased investigation by the USDA Office of the Inspector
	General and an end to the use of U.S. taxpayer funds for the research.

An additional 118 unique comments were received.

- 20 comments were received in support of the US MARC Facility and its research.
- 98 in general, encouraged USDA to: close the facility; provide more robust site reviews, including the pending review by the Office of the Inspector General; and end the use of tax payer funds for the private meat industry.
- One commenter requested clarification on industry standards for swine pens.
- One commenter identified a discrepancy in the report related to the date of Dr. John Clifford's site visit.

Verbal Comments

- A total of 8 verbal comments were received.
- 1 commenter asked for clarification on a statement in the report on industry standards for swine pens (page 4).
- Three commenters supported the US MARC facility and identified the benefits of the research that has been completed at the facility.
- Four commenters asked for additional review and oversight:
  - For the ongoing research at US MARC to be reviewed by a second IACUC committee;
  - For USDA to apply the Animal Welfare Act to all research at US MARC and other USDA Facilities;
  - For the Animal and Plant Health Inspection Service (APHIS) to implement and perform rigorous inspections;
  - Additional accountability on the research within ARS; and
  - Additional unannounced site visits.

In conclusion, the independent panel made five general edits to the report based on the comments received.

- Corrected the date of Dr. John Clifford's site visit.
- Identified the Ag Guide as their only reference for identifying the appropriate size of swine pens.
- Added additional information on the visual cues used to identify animal health and well-being.
- Added additional information on the details of the site visit.
- Added information on changes to the IACUC review process at USMARC that were implemented in December 2014.

In: The Animal Welfare Act and Farm Animal ... ISBN: 978-1-63484-380-5
Editor: Albert V. Griffin

Chapter 4

FINAL REPORT: FINDINGS AND RECOMMENDATIONS ON THE PHASE II REVIEW OF THE ANIMAL CARE AND WELL-BEING AT THE AGRICULTURAL RESEARCH SERVICE TO THE REE UNDER SECRETARY*

Agricultural Research Service

BACKGROUND

The Agricultural Research Service (ARS) Animal Handling and Welfare Review Panel (ARS-AHWRP) was established under the authority of section 1409A(e) of the National Agricultural Research, Extension, and Teaching Policy Act, as amended (7 U.S.C. 3124a(e)), to review ARS agency-wide research animal care and well-being policies, procedures, and standards for agricultural livestock in ARS research. This review consists of two phases: Phase I includes an immediate review of the U.S. Meat Animal Research Center (USMARC) to be completed in 60 days; Phase II charges the panel

* This is an edited, reformatted and augmented version of a report issued by the United States Department of Agriculture, July 23, 2015.

with reviewing additional 3-5 ARS locations where livestock research is conducted. This report focuses on Phase II of the charge.

In regards to ARS facilities using animals in research, the ARS-AHWRP was charged to:

1) Visit 3-5 ARS locations where livestock research is conducted.
2) Inspect facilities, pens, fields, etc., where animals are housed or involved in experimentation.
3) Review the composition of each location's Institutional Animal Care and Use Committee (IACUC), records of its meetings, and evidence of compliance with agency P&Ps.
4) Review processes used to select and evaluate experimental designs and protocols under the IACUC at each location.
5) Assess care and well-being training needs for staff having responsibility for handling animals at each location.
6) Prepare a draft report for the Under Secretary that summarizes findings for each site visited, and generalized for ARS agency-wide; reaches conclusions as to whether the care and handling of animals and the capacity of facilities and staff at each location are in compliance with institutional P&Ps and industry standards, taking into account that ARS has a research mission, not a production mission; make location-specific and agency-wide recommendations to improve compliance, if necessary, with institutional P&Ps and industry standards; and make recommendations, if appropriate, for changes to institutional P&Ps providing oversight of livestock animal care in ARS's research settings.

The ARS-AHWRP is made up of four members and one ex-officio member appointed by the Secretary of Agriculture: Dr. Aaron Olsen, Chair (Director, Laboratory Animal Research Center, Utah State University); Dr. Lonny Dixon (Director/Attending Veterinarian, Office of Animal Resources, University of Missouri); Dr. Stephen Ford (Endowed Professor, University of Wyoming); Dr. Mo Salman (Professor and Director, Animal Population Health Institute at Colorado State University); and Dr. John Clifford, Ex-Officio Member (Chief Veterinary Officer, USDA, Animal and Plant Health Inspection Service (APHIS)).

In compliance with its charge, the ARS-AHWRP members visited 5 ARS locations using animals in research for Phase II of this review. Brief summaries of the site visits, including dates, panel members present, facility overview, the composition and function of the IACUC, and research site-specific comments and recommendations are below. Although some of these site visits were limited to 2-3 panel members, the site visit reports were shared with all panel members for the final recommendations.

SITE VISIT METHODOLOGY

ARS locations were independently selected by the panel members based upon a review of all ARS facilities where animal research is conducted. The intention was to select sites with diversity in their missions and experiments. Factors considered in selecting sites were geographic location, co-location with other research institutions (such as a college or university), the number and type of animals used at each facility, and the nature of the research being conducted. The panel members recognized the highly diverse nature of research programs supported by ARS, and sites were selected in an effort to evaluate a broad spectrum of research and animal care programs. Preference was given to facilities with larger animal care programs based on the presumption that this would provide the best opportunity for panel members to directly observe animal care and handling and associated research activities.

Prior to each visit, the location was requested to have the following documents available for review:

- Last 3-4 IACUC meeting minutes
- Last 2 IACUC semi-annual facility inspection reports
- Representative sampling of IACUC protocols (or equivalent document)
- If an external IACUC is conducting protocol reviews, any MOUs with that organization/university
- Standard operating procedures regarding IACUC function and protocol review; animal husbandry, welfare, and veterinary care
- Animal Health records

Each site visit consisted of an inspection of facilities and direct observation of animals and animal handling, interviews with researchers and key members of the animal care team, and review of documents relevant to animal use and care.

In the course of facility inspections, priority was given to areas where animals were currently being housed and panel members had the opportunity to directly observe the handling and care of research animals in those facilities.

Group and individual interviews were conducted at each location. These interviews focused on identifying how the IACUC functioned at each location, including how protocols were reviewed and approved or disapproved. Individuals in key positions were interviewed at each location, including the ARS Center Director or Research Leader, the Attending Veterinarian, ARS researchers, members of the animal care team, the IACUC chair, and members of the IACUC. At some locations, the support scientists and technicians were also interviewed.

At all sites, the documentation review included standard operating procedures (SOPs) or equivalent documents guiding both animal care and IACUC actions, any written cooperative agreements between the ARS facility and associated research institutions, applications submitted to the IACUC for review and approval detailing animal research activities (e.g., IACUC Protocols), and facility inspection reports. The documents reviewed were based upon requests by the ARS-AHWRP members.

In conducting the review of SOPs and IACUC protocols, all such documents were readily made available to the panel members for review. In accordance with its charge, the panel focused its review efforts on current and active research projects, and all current and active research protocols were made available for review. Priority was given to those activities and protocols that had the potential for increased pain and distress of research animals, such as research involving surgery or infectious diseases.

During interviews and review of documents, the panel also reviewed training programs and records for individuals involved in animal care.

At the conclusion of each site visit, the ARS-AHWRP members conducted an "exit interview" with representatives of the ARS facility. This provided an opportunity for the panel to present an overview of its findings, emphasize areas of strengths observed, highlight areas for improvements or gaps in the animal oversight process, and include a dialogue about how the location could improve its processes in the context of each individual animal care program.

LOCATION REVIEWS

Livestock and Range Research Laboratory

Miles City, Montana
Date of Site Visit: May 13, 2015
Panel Members Present: Aaron Olsen, Mo Salman

Facility Summary

The Livestock and Range Research Laboratory (LARRL) is located at Fort Keogh, near Miles City, Montana. The research facility is focused exclusively on beef cattle, particularly in the context of pasture and range grazing management systems. All animals used at the LARRL are owned and managed by Montana State University (MSU), while experiments are conducted by LARRL staff. The relationship between LARRL and MSU is governed by a written Memorandum of Agreement.

The Institutional Animal Care and Use Committee (IACUC) consists of six voting members, including a local, private veterinarian and a local religious leader. The local veterinarian serves as the Attending Veterinarian on the IACUC and provides veterinary care and oversight for the facility on a fee for service basis. He has provided veterinary care for the LARRL for over 20 years.

The research site consists of over 80 square miles of rangeland. The site visit included inspections of several outlying range areas with animals, animal handling areas, and observation of animals being handled as part of a research project.

It is the opinion of the panel members that all animals observed were healthy and well cared for. This conclusion is based upon the direct observation of the animals, noting the overall appearance and condition of animals. The physical facilities were adequate and appropriate for the nature of the research being conducted. The observation of animal handling showed individuals with skill and care in working with the animals. The IACUC was found to be properly constituted and in compliance with ARS Policies and Procedures. The IACUC appeared to be functioning as ARS Policies and Procedures would intend.

Strengths of the LARRL Animal Care Program

- All animals observed appear to be well cared for and healthy.
- The IACUC meets the standards established in both the *Guide* and the *Ag Guide,* and is thus compliant with ARS Policies and Procedures.
- LARRL and MSU have a clearly written Memorandum of Agreement which details the arrangements between LARRL and MSU, including the oversight of animal use by the IACUC. Additionally, representatives of the MSU IACUC visited LARRL prior to the completion of the memorandum and found the IACUC function to be consistent with the standards of MSU.
- There is evidence of good communication between LARRL and MSU in regards to animal use oversight. This communication was highlighted by the presence of a MSU representative at the AWHRP site visit, despite the distance of over 140 miles from the Billings, Montana campus.
- The veterinarian was fully engaged in all aspects of veterinary care and was, by all reports, providing high quality veterinary care.
- The IACUC members and animal care staff had records of training and recent Beef Quality.
- Assurance Certification. The institution has recently begun using the CITI online training modules as a component of its animal care training program.
- The IACUC community member was highly engaged and expressed a feeling of being fully vested in the IACUC functions.
- Contact information for veterinary care and IACUC representatives were clearly posted in animal handling areas.
- IACUC meeting minutes showed evidence of discussion and resolution of animal health issues as they arose.

Recommendations for the LARRL Animal Care Program

- The panel members are of the opinion that the LARRL is a well-run facility, and the IACUC is both properly constituted and functioning as intended. We offer the following recommendations as potential refinements to the existing processes in place:
- The IACUC bylaws or other standard operating procedure documents should clearly state the authority of the Attending Veterinarian to

oversee all aspects of animal well-being, including the authority diagnose disease, prescribe treatment, and, especially, to remove an animal from a study and/or euthanize an animal, if necessary, according to the professional opinion of the Attending Veterinarian.

- A written process or policy for how the IACUC will respond to concerns about animal welfare should be available.
- Clarification is needed for the procedure of how and when the IACUC will make use of the Designated Member Review (DMR) process for review and approval of IACUC protocols.
- Clearly state that protocols not covered by the Animal Welfare Act must be fully reviewed and approved by the committee at least once every three years for ongoing protocols. At this time all research protocols at the LARRL would fall under the non-AWA covered category and can be eligible for up to a three year approval.
- Clarify the authority of the IACUC to suspend ongoing research activities when the committee votes to do so by a majority of a quorum present.
- A copy of an appropriate "whistleblower" policy should be posted in animal handling facilities.
- An expanded use of standard operating procedures (SOPs) or equivalent documents for some aspects of animal handling or veterinary care should be available. Common procedures, such as pregnancy detection using an ultrasound, may be appropriately detailed in a SOP, which in turn may be referenced within an IACUC protocol using that procedure.
- Establish a clear method to include minority opinions in semi-annual inspection and IACUC meetings. Meeting minutes can include a section for minority opinion, even if left blank due to the absence of a minority opinion.
- Seek additional opportunities for training of IACUC members via conferences, webinars, etc.

LIVESTOCK BEHAVIOR RESEARCH UNIT

West Lafayette, Indiana
Panel Members Present: Aaron Olsen, Mo Salman Date(s) of Site Visit: May 15, 2015

Facility Summary

- The Livestock Behavior Research Unit (LBRU) is co-located with Purdue University in West Lafayette, Indiana. The LBRU emphasis is research aiming to improve welfare of livestock animals by focusing on animal behavior to develop best animal care practices.
- The Purdue University farms are accredited by the Association for Assessment and Accreditation for Laboratory Animal Care (AAALAC) International. The LBRU is fully integrated into the Purdue University animal care program. The vast majority of animals used are owned by Purdue University. Almost all animal handling is conducted in Purdue owned facilities, with the exception of a large animal room owed by ARS (which is also included in the AAALAC accreditation). Researchers at the LBRU carry adjunct faculty status with Purdue University, which allows them to use University resources in the same manner as regular University faculty. LBRU researchers and staff members are required to meet the same training requirements as Purdue University faculty and staff members, and documentation of training and qualifications of personnel is maintained by the Purdue Animal Care and Use Committee (PACUC) office.
- The panel members visited the Purdue dairy and swine holding facilities. At the time of the site visit only a limited number of animals were involved in LBRU directed research, although the sites visited had been used for ARS sponsored research in the past and are expected to be involved in future ARS projects. All animals observed appeared healthy and well cared for. The physical facilities were well maintained and were adequate for all research and animal handling needs.
- Purdue University features a properly constituted and robustly functioning animal oversight committee (the PACUC) which reviews all animal research at Purdue, including ARS sponsored research conducted by LBRU personnel. In the past, LBRU researchers have served on the PACUC and may do so again in the future.
- It is the opinion of the panel members that research conducted at the LBRU is fully compliant with both the letter and the spirit of ARS Policies and Procedures in regards to animal care and oversight.

Strengths of the LBRU Animal Care Program

- All animals observed appear to be well cared for and healthy.
- The IACUC meets the standards established in both the Guide and the Ag Guide, and is thus compliant with ARS Policies and Procedures.
- As noted above, the entire animal care program at Purdue University is AAALAC accredited. This is highly commendable and demonstrates a commitment to animal health and welfare by both LBRU personnel and Purdue University.
- The relationship between LBRU and Purdue University may represent a potential model for other ARS facilities to meet the animal use oversight requirements.

Recommendations for the LBRU Animal Care Program

At this time the panel members do not have any recommendations specifically for the LBRU and its University partner, Purdue. We continue to note the opportunity and need within ARS to share best practices for animal care and handling as well as the challenges and solutions associated with animal oversight between ARS units. We believe that due to its strong oversight model in association with Purdue University, and in particular because of the LBRU research focus on animal welfare, this unit may be in a position to play a leadership role in promoting best animal welfare practices across ARS facilities.

SOUTHEAST POULTRY RESEARCH LABORATORY

Athens, Georgia
Panel Members Present: Mo Salman, Lonny Dixon Date(s) of Site Visit: June 15-16, 2015

Facility Summary

The Southeast Poultry Research Laboratory (SEPRL), located in Athens, GA, is a research laboratory focusing exclusively on avian diseases, particularly infectious bacterial and viral diseases. The facility includes production units of eggs and live birds exclusive for experiments, biosafety laboratory level (BSL) 2, and BSL-3. The production unit includes specific-pathogen-free (SPF) eggs and birds. All animals used at the SEPRL are owned and managed by ARS with the ability to collaborate with other scientists using the facility under the authority and supervision of the researchers from SEPRL. The facility is within a complex that is currently being reorganized with the Russell B. Russell Agricultural Research Center to form the U.S. National Poultry Research Center.

The Institutional Animal Care and Use Committee consists of 7 voting members, including two local community representatives, who act as alternates for one another. Veterinary care is provided by a designated full-time attending veterinarian who also contributes to hands-on training with a certification process. In the absence of the Attending Veterinarian (AV) at SEPRL, the Attending Veterinarian delegates the responsibilities for animals in writing to another veterinarian of the facility to ensure that adequate veterinary care is provided at all times.

The site visit included a tour of several buildings in which birds (chickens and turkeys) were housed. Animal handlers and animal technicians were interviewed in addition to the leading scientists, researchers, and support scientists/technicians, and IACUC members.

It is the opinion of the two panel members that participated in this visit that all birds observed (three SPF flocks and several BSL-2 study birds) were healthy and well cared for and there was no evidence of animal mistreatment. The physical facilities were aged and in need of constant repair and judged marginal by the site visitors for the type of infectious research conducted. While the state of the physical facilities did not present a concern in regards to animal welfare, inadequate biocontainment facilities can present a risk to facility employees. Processes and procedures were in place to allow safe and biosecured research to continue for the time being. The observation of animal handling showed individuals with skill and care in working with these birds. The IACUC was found to be properly constituted, in full compliance with ARS Policies and Procedures, and appeared to be functioning as intended.

Strengths of the SEPRL Animal Care Program

- All animals observed appear to be well cared for and healthy.
- The IACUC meets the standards established in both the *Guide* and the *Ag Guide,* and is thus compliant with ARS Policies and Procedures.
- The animal care and use program at SEPRL has a current assurance (#A4298-01) with the National Institutes of Health, Office of Laboratory Animal Welfare (OLAW) that will expire May 31, 2018.
- SEPRL maintains a strong functioning IACUC that was established over 20 years ago. The IACUC composition complies with regulatory requirements. The IACUC chair and its entire members were highly engaged and expressed a feeling of being fully vested in the IACUC functions. There appears to be a fully engaged community member and alternate community member. The IACUC functions meet compliance requirements of the *Guide* and the Animal Welfare Act. Humane endpoints are required for all protocols and are strictly adhered to.
- Training of scientists, technicians, animal care staff, and IACUC members is excellent and extensive and includes hands-on training and proficiency demonstration for all animal procedures. Training is well documented.
- There is evidence of excellent communication between IACUC members, researchers and animal care personnel in regards to animal use and oversight.
- The attending veterinarian was fully engaged in all aspects of veterinary care and was, by all reports, providing high quality hands-on training and veterinary care.

Recommendations for the SEPRL Animal Care Program

The panel members are of the opinion that the SEPRL is a well-run facility with high quality of research and the IACUC is both properly constituted and functioning as intended. We offer the following recommendations as potential refinements to the existing processes in place:

- Although the hands-on training program is excellent for the facility employees, independent recognition of its certificate should be explored through neighboring universities such as University of Georgia (UGA).

- Upgrades and/or replacement of aged BSL-2, BSL-3, and breeding facilities is critical for SEPRL to meet its research goals. ARS needs to recognize the importance of improving these facilities and provide adequate resources to support these functions. Monies have been allocated to renovate and replace some facilities. However, significant additional monies are required to complete the overall facilities improvement needs.
- Because of the focus on infectious disease research at SEPRL, a particularly important consideration is to reevaluate the pay grade level of biosafety professionals so that qualified professionals can be recruited and retained.
- IACUC operation requires administrative support in its daily operation and should not be left to the chair to handle all of the required documentation;
- Although the "whistleblower" policy is known to the staff members who were interviewed, the IACUC is encouraged to post the availability of this option to all employees in the various buildings of SEPRL.
- It was announced during our site visit that both SEPRL and RRC would be under the leadership of one Center Director. This may be an ideal opportunity to consolidate and harmonize IACUC and other compliance activities (i.e., biosafety officer) between sites using common resources. Combining IACUC functions would allow efficient use of resources and provide the opportunity for administrative support for the joint IACUC.

Richard B. Russell Agricultural Research Center

Athens, Georgia

Panel Members Present: Mo Salman, Lonny Dixon Date(s) of Site Visit: June 15-16, 2015

Facility Summary

The Richard B. Russell Agricultural Research Center (RRC), located in Athens, GA, is a research laboratory focusing exclusively on avian products including safety and quality. The facility includes 5 research units: Egg Safety & Quality, Quality & Safety Assessment, Toxicology & Mycotoxin, Poultry Microbiological Safety & Processing, and Bacterial Epidemiology & Antimicrobial Resistance. Research activities in some of these units are not engaged with live birds. Birds are supplied to the Center either from commercial sources or the UGA, there were presently no breeder flocks housed. The birds are supplied by UGA through a Memorandum of Understanding. Laboratory mice are maintained within the Center for specific research activities with mycotoxin.

The IACUC consists of nine voting members, including a community member who is also an employee of a maintenance contractor with the center. Some of the veterinary care is provided by the veterinarian who serves as a member of the IACUC but they do not serve as the Attending Veterinarian. All scientists engaged in using live animals for their research are requested to be members of IACUC. The chair of the IACUC provides training at UGA on euthanasia of poultry. Student trainees receive a university approved certification after completion of the training. Facility inspections and program reviews were completed but not of the frequency required by regulations.

The site visit included tours of the building in which mice are housed, the pilot poultry slaughter plant, and an offsite building used to house live birds. Demonstrations of various stunning and euthanasia methods were performed as part of the site visit. Scientists, animal handlers, and IACUC members were interviewed.

It is the opinion of the two panel members that participated in this visit that all experimental animals observed were healthy and appeared well cared for. The physical facilities for housing live poultry were adequate and appropriate for the nature of the research being conducted. The pilot poultry processing plant was well maintained, clean, and functional. The area used for housing mice requires some modifications to meet the intent of the *Guide*. Leadership and staff members were aware of the needs and a plan for the facility modifications is currently approved and funded.

The IACUC consisted of scientists, non-scientists, a chair, a veterinarian, and a community representative, as required by ARS policies and procedures. However, the community representative was employed by a service company contracted to provide maintenance for the facility. While this meets the definition of a non-affiliated or community representative, it is the opinion of the panel that the individual's employment may be viewed as contingent upon continuation of the facility maintenance contract, therefore, there may not be sufficient separation from the facility to fully meet the spirit of having a non-affiliated community representative.

Strengths of the RRC Animal Care Program

- All animals observed appear to be well cared for and healthy.
- The IACUC meets the standards established in both the *Guide* and the *Ag Guide,* and is thus compliant with ARS Policies and Procedures.
- In spite of less emphasis on the use or need of live animals in research, all the scientists who are engaged in the use of live animals are members of the IACUC;
- There is good scientific interaction between the Center and UGA. This is manifested by interinstitutional transfer of birds from UGA protocols to RRC protocols.
- There is a link to UGA in certifying training individuals/employees in euthanasia of birds. This type of independent recognition of the training program is encouraged.

Recommendations for the RRC Animal Care Program

The two panel members are of the opinion that the RRC is a well-run facility with high quality of research. We offer the following recommendations as potential refinements to the existing processes in place:

- There is a need to appoint an attending veterinarian that is fully engaged in all aspects of veterinary care as defined in the Animal Welfare Act and the *Guide*.
- The IACUC community member is employed by a company that provides contract maintenance and support services to RRC. It is recommended that the community member be completely unaffiliated with the RRC.
- IACUC functions, as required by the Animal Welfare Act and the *Guide*, should be reviewed and the activities of the IACUC should be

increased to be compliant, including facility inspections, program review, and animal care and use protocols.

- Rodent housing facilities should be evaluated for appropriateness for future intended mycotoxin work. Animal rooms currently have a positive pressure differential to the hallways and not all surfaces are impervious to moisture and readily decontaminated. Some mice were routinely housed in wire bottom cages. Whenever possible, mice should be socially housed in solid bottom cages with bedding and appropriate environmental enrichment. Exceptions to these requirements can be made for scientific reasons, if approved by the IACUC.
- Although the "whistleblower" policy is known to the staff members who were interviewed, the IACUC is encouraged to post the availability of this option to all employees in the various floors and offsite building of RRC.
- It was announced during our site visit that both SEPRL and RRC would be under the leadership of one Center Director. This may be an ideal opportunity to consolidate and harmonize IACUC and other compliance activities (i.e., biosafety officer) between sites using common resources. Combining IACUC functions would allow efficient use of resources and provide the opportunity for administrative support for the joint IACUC.

National Animal Disease Center

Ames, Iowa
Panel Members Present: Aaron Olsen, Mo Salman, Lonny Dixon, Stephen Ford
Date(s) of Site Visit: June 17-19, 2015

Facility Summary

The National Centers for Animal Health (NCAH), located in Ames Iowa, is a multi-center facility consisting of the National Veterinary Services Laboratory (NVSL), the Center of Veterinary Biologics (CVB), and the National Animal Disease Center (NADC). Of these units, the NVSL and the CVB are components of the Animal and Plant Health Inspection Service,

Veterinary Services (APHIS, VS) while the NADC is operated by the ARS. NCAH animal holding facilities serves ARS and APHIS for their research needs. At the current time, one IACUC serves the ARS program while a separate IACUC serves the needs of the two APHIS units. However, NCAH operates a single animal care program serving both APHIS and ARS units, which is operated solely by ARS staff members. The APHIS and shared components of NCAH animal care and use program is currently accredited by AAALAC, although the ARS components are not similarly accredited. The site members visited and observed areas holding animals associated with ARS research projects, but did not observe areas holding animals used exclusively for APHIS supported research projects. With the exception of veterinary and animal care staff that serve both ARS and APHIS, APHIS staff did not participate in the site review.

The research programs at the NADC focuses primarily on infectious diseases with the potential to impact livestock. As such, a substantial number of the animals are housed under BSL-2 or BSL-3 conditions. The animal care program at NADC is unique in that it makes use of multiple atypical research species, such as bison, elk, raccoons, and white tailed deer, in addition to domestic livestock species and rodents.

During the site visit panel members observed (either directly or via video camera) all areas holding research animals, including outdoor pastures and pens, indoor infectious disease laboratories, and a rodent vivarium.

The ARS IACUC was considered to be properly constituted and in compliance with ARS Policies and Procedures. The IACUC included 11 voting members, including the Attending Veterinarian who oversaw the animal care program, a community member, and research scientists and technicians. In addition, the IACUC was supported by an administrative staff member acting as an IACUC Administrator.

It is the opinion of the panel members that research animals observed appeared healthy and well cared for. There was no observable evidence of misuse or abuse. Furthermore, it was noted that substantial efforts had been made to identify best practices when working with atypical animal species. The small animal vivarium and the relatively new BSL-3 large animal holding facility may be considered exceptionally good facilities while other animal holding areas would be considered adequate. The physical facilities did not negatively impact animal welfare. However, it was noted that some facilities were limited in their ability to provide enhanced animal welfare, such as organic bedding material in large animal BSL-2 facilities, due to limitations of plumbing and other infrastructure to handle bedding waste. The animal care staff is aware of these limitations and is routinely seeking ways to mitigate the limitations imposed by physical facilities.

Strengths of the NADC Animal Care Program

- All animals appear to be well cared for and healthy.
- The IACUC meets the standards established in both the *Guide* and the *Ag Guide,* and is thus compliant with ARS Policies and Procedures. The community representative was present at our meeting and appeared fully engaged in the IACUC review process.
- The animal care program is managed by highly engaged and knowledgeable animal care staff, including the veterinarians and the IACUC administrator.
- Extensive efforts have been made to develop best practices for working with atypical research species. In particular, the innovative animal enrichment program and the white-tailed deer breeding program deserve special note.
- Review of animal care protocols found evidence of well-developed humane endpoints, particularly for animals involved in infectious disease research.
- The animal care and use program at NADC has a current assurance with the National Institutes of Health, Office of Laboratory Animal Welfare (OLAW).

Recommendations for the NADC Animal Care Program

The panel members are of the opinion that the NADC is a well-run facility, and the IACUC is both properly constituted and functioning as intended. We offer the following recommendations as potential refinements to the existing processes in place:

- A research veterinarian should not also fill the role of Attending Veterinarian for treatment or handling animals beyond the required research protocol. In some instances, IACUC protocols listed the researcher (who is also a veterinarian) as the only contact for veterinary care issues. Although individuals may be fully qualified as a researcher, they should not act as his or her own attending veterinarian as such a situation removes the appropriate oversight role of a veterinarian. This does not limit the ability of a researcher who is a veterinarian from providing any required care, but it does necessitate that animal health issues be communicated to the veterinary staff providing oversight.

- Animal use protocols should include more robust justifications for the number of animals requested for research projects. Multiple methods may be used to establish that justification, including power analysis, previously published research, or specific experimental design requirements.
- Animal care contact information and copies of whistleblower policies should be more broadly posted. Many, but not all, animal facilities included postings of such information.
- Train all staff on site on how to report welfare concerns. NADC makes use of a private security firm to provide on-site security, including monitoring cameras in some animal holding areas. Explicit training of all staff, including contract security personnel, on how to report animal welfare or illness concerns would broaden the ability of animal care staff to learn of potential illness or injury.
- A research technician serving as IACUC chair is less than ideal. It was noted that the current chair of the IACUC is a research technician. Although the engagement of research technicians and animal handlers in IACUC composition is encouraged, the ideal chair of the committee should be an individual with in-depth experience in research animals and sufficient stature and standing within the local research community to help implement a robust animal care program.
- The opportunity for IACUC members to serve more than a single 3-year term on the committee and committee chairs more than a single one-year term, should be considered. It was noted that IACUC members routinely served a single 3-year term on the committee before rotating off, and chairs serve a single one-year term in the chairmanship. This arrangement is intended to limit intellectual stagnation within the committee. However, a mix of newer and more experience committee members may be ideal. The opportunity for committee members to serve two or three consecutive terms can be beneficial in providing continuity in IACUC functions. Similarly for the chair position, an extended appointment can allow a chair to both

understand the needs of an animal care program and develop and implement program improvements.

- Additional and ongoing training of all IACUC members is strongly encouraged. Multiple training opportunities currently exist in the form of literature, webcasts and webinars, and training conferences. It is the opinion of the panel that in-person training opportunities, such as IACUC 101 meetings, are the preferred option, when possible.
- Consideration should be given to combining IACUCs and other oversight functions between ARS and APHIS research teams. The APHIS research units and the ARS research unit maintain separate IACUCs, although there is a single animal care program, and the IACUC administrator and Attending Veterinarian serve concurrently on both committees. The panel recognizes that the APHIS and ARS research units have different missions and goals. However, we suggest that combining the IACUCs be considered as it is the opinion of the panel that this would introduce efficiencies in the IACUC process and help ensure that expectations of animal care at the site are consistent across all units.

AGENCY WIDE FINDINGS AND RECOMMENDATIONS

ARS Policies and Procedures

ARS Policies and Procedures number 635.1, *Humane Animal Care and Use,* identifies *The Guide for the Care and Use of Agricultural Animals in Research and Teaching* (the Ag Guide), produced by the Federation of Animal Science Societies, as the primary document guiding the use of agricultural animals at ARS sites, and *The Guide for the Care and Use of Laboratory Animals* (The Guide) as the primary guiding document for the care of non-agricultural animals. The Guide and the Ag Guide serve as a vital reference documents for the care and oversight of animals used in research for ARS. The panel, therefore, strongly supports the use of the current iterations of the Guide (Eighth Edition, 2011) and the Ag Guide (Third Edition, 2010) as the guiding documents in regards to care and use of animals at ARS facilities.

Animal Care and Handling within ARS

It is the strong opinion of the panel that there was no evidence for misuse or abuse of animals at the ARS sites visited. Interactions with veterinarians and animal care staff found individuals committed to the health and well-being of the animals under their care. Direct observations of animals found the animals to be healthy in appearance, well fed, and with no external signs of injury or abuse. When able to observe the handling of animals, the panel found individuals who exhibit care and professionalism in working with all species.

Animal Research Oversight within ARS

Finding 1

The role and expectations of the Institutional Animal Care and Use Committee and Attending Veterinarian is not uniformly understood at all ARS sites.

The panel members have observed a variety of models for implementing an effective animal care oversight program and a robustly functioning IACUC. The models observed have ranged from complete integration of an ARS research unit into the animal care program of a co-located academic institution (as observed with the Livestock Behavioral Research Unit located with Purdue University), to a complete stand-alone IACUC and animal care program (as observed at the National Animal Disease Center in Ames, Iowa). The other sites visited had varying degrees of interaction with associated academic institutions. It is the opinion of the panel that any of these oversight models can fully meet the expectations for research oversight and high quality animal care. Indeed, due to the *diverse nature of ARS research centers it is important that individual sites be allowed flexibility to meet the oversight requirements within the context of their specific size and organizational structure and to meet their specific research missions.*

A primary function of the IACUC is to act as an agent for the welfare and wellbeing of animals used in research. To properly fulfill this function, the committee members must fully understand the role and importance of the IACUC. In particular, the Attending Veterinarian plays a crucial role in promoting animal welfare. The panel, however, has noted inconsistencies in the understanding of the roles, expectations, and functioning of the IACUC and its members. This may, in part, be attributed to the nature of small and isolated research sites where individuals are required to divide time and attention between multiple, divergent responsibilities.

Recommendation 1

ARS should work to harmonize expectations of the IACUC across all sites using animals in research. To accomplish this recommendation, the panel suggests:

- Explicitly state the roles, responsibilities, and authority of the IACUC and Attending Veterinarian in ARS Policies and Procedures.
- Provide adequate administrative and financial support for an IACUC to complete its assigned functions.
- Provide expanded training opportunities both within and without ARS on the role and function of an IACUC.
- Develop means for greater communication both between ARS units and with institutions outside of ARS to expand understanding of the proper role and function of an IACUC.
- ARS sites cooperating or collaborating with academic or other research institutions should do so under clearly written agreements that include requirements for animal welfare oversight.

For an IACUC to fulfill its welfare and oversight functions, it is vital to have adequate administrative and financial support. It is beyond the purview of the review panel to set specific guidelines for support and each research site will have unique needs. *We, therefore, encourage facility directors to make animal welfare oversight responsibilities a priority when considering budgetary needs, and providing strong administrative support to individuals tasked with participating in oversight activities.*

The expectations of an IACUC have become somewhat standardized at academic and industry research institutions, while still providing sufficient flexibility to accommodate different research emphases within a wide variety of research programs. Consequently, a wide variety of training resources have become available for individuals involved in the activities of animal research oversight. The panel emphasizes the need for adequate training of all IACUC members, but especially committee chairs and Attending Veterinarians as these individuals carry special responsibilities in regards to animal welfare oversight. It is not the role of the panel to prescribe specific training programs that must be followed. But based on the experience of several panel members, the IACUC 101 training conferences presented by the organization Public Responsibility in Medicine and Research (PRIM&R) are highly recommended for members of IACUCs at ARS sites.

In addition to enhanced training of IACUC members, increased communication between individuals associated with animal welfare oversight across the ARS organization can provide great benefit to ensuring consistency and quality of animal care and oversight programs across ARS. This type of communication will permit dissemination of effective techniques for operating a robust IACUC and meeting all other animal research oversight requirements. The chairs of the IACUC committees across all ARS location are encouraged to establish regular communications in order to share experiences and policy implementation practices. For example, the biosafety officers in ARS meet regularly to share best practices and updated policies and procedures.

Due to the broad and diverse nature of research programs at academic institutions, they often have well established and robust animal oversight organizations already in place. Where appropriate, the panel encourages ongoing and even enhanced cooperative and collaborative efforts between ARS and academic research institutions, both in fields of scientific inquiry and in fulfilling animal welfare oversight activities. Where ARS sites do cooperate with academic or other research institutions in sharing oversight responsibilities, ARS members are encouraged to serve on IACUCs both to provide input to the committee function and to gain valuable experience in the appropriate function of an IACUC.

Finding 2

Service on oversight committees, such as the IACUC, may be viewed by some ARS employees as a diversion from overall job duties.

Institution oversight committees, such as the IACUC, serve vital functions to the operations of research organizations. The IACUC in particular provides a means for oversight of animal welfare. Ideally, the IACUC can also help promote high quality, scientific efforts by encouraging researchers to refine their research technique, experimental goals, and experimental design early in the process of developing an experiment. For an IACUC to function well and meet its ideal operation, it requires a substantial time commitment on the part of all committee members, but especially on the part of the Attending Veterinarian and the IACUC chair. This time is required to adequately understand the IACUC processes as well as the proposed research activities. However, in conversation with researchers and other ARS staff members, participation on the IACUC is not adequately considered during performance evaluations, and the time required to perform oversight functions is not considered when evaluating research output. Consequently, ARS employees may view service on an IACUC as a diversion from research duties, or worse, a hindrance to achieving personal and professional goals.

Recommendation 2

Participation in research oversight activities, such as service on IACUCs, should be an important part of an individual's career development path. Such service should be appropriately considered and recognized during routine personnel evaluations and as part of considerations for advancement or promotion.

The time commitment necessary to fulfill oversight responsibilities has the potential to impact other employment duties, such as research output by scientists. This consideration may make some ARS employees reluctant to serve on the committee, or limit their engagement on a committee when serving. By acknowledging, and appropriately recognizing the value of oversight committee service, the ARS administration will help emphasize the vital role such committees play in serving their research communities. Furthermore, including oversight committee service as a key component in an individual's career development within ARS can have the benefits of encouraging highly capable individuals to serve and engage with oversight activities, and can help educate ARS scientists and other staff members on the important role that these oversight committees play in supporting research activities.

Physical Facilities and Equipment

ARS operates multiple research locations across many states. Oftentimes these sites are geographically isolated from other research institutions due to the nature of the research being conducted. This arrangement provides both unique opportunities and challenges. The opportunities arise from the ability to address research needs targeted at specific user groups and stakeholders in various branches of the agriculture industries. The challenges arise from the need to maintain facilities ranging from complex integrated biosafety laboratories to extensive outdoor pasture and rangeland.

It is the opinion of the panel that in most instances the physical facilities were adequate for the research being conducted, and in some instances physical facilities were excellent. However, the advancing age of some facilities was apparent. Individuals at research sites were aware of the limitations of existing animal facilities and were actively seeking innovative means to achieve research goals in existing facilities. Maintaining aging facilities will become an increasingly difficult challenge, and long range plans must include consideration for significant upgrade or replacement of existing facilities if ARS is to continue to meet its research mission in regards to animal agriculture.

Recommendation 3

Adequate funding should be provided to maintain current facilities, and to upgrade or replace aging facilities. ARS fulfills a vital research role in support of agriculture and public health. Among its unique strengths is the ability to implement and maintain long-term research projects. Physical facilities are a key component in the ability of ARS to meet its research goals, particularly in areas such as infectious disease research which require intensive physical facilities to safely perform the research. While facilities are currently adequate, failure to maintain and eventually upgrade or replace aging facilities may eventually limit research capabilities at ARS sites.

Animal Handling and Veterinary Care

Finding 3

Individuals within ARS display appropriate and sometimes exceptionally good animal handling and care. However, there is limited opportunity to disseminate best animal care practices between ARS facilities or to the broader research and agricultural communities.

As indicated previously, it is the opinion of the panel members that individuals working with animals routinely displayed care and professionalism in completing their animal handling duties. Indeed, there were several instances where individuals had developed improvements and refinements to animal care handling practices that enhance overall animal welfare. When such efforts and actions occur they are highly commendable. Furthermore, some sites, such as the U.S. Meat Animal Research Center, had developed internal criteria for recognizing skill in animal care providers, while others, such as the RRC, had provided opportunity to receive some training and certification outside of the research facility. However, these arrangements to recognize excellent knowledge and skill in animal care appear to be the exception rather than the standard.

Recommendation 4

ARS should provide means for animal care staff to share innovations and best practices both within and without the ARS organization. Concurrent with sharing best practices ARS should develop means to identify and appropriately recognize individuals who provide exceptionally good animal care and/or develop unique and innovative techniques which lead to improved animal welfare.

It is beyond the scope of the panel's charge to determine the exact means by which best practices can be shared between ARS sites, and between ARS and the broader agricultural and research communities. However, the panel notes that multiple organizations exist which focus on the enhancement of care for animals involved in research. These existing organizations may provide an outlet for sharing of animal care practices, or may serve as a model for how to organize and disseminate animal care techniques.

In addition to providing avenues for sharing best animal care practices, veterinary and animal care staff should be actively encouraged to share best practices and innovative animal care techniques. The panel members recognize that the primary role of animal care and veterinary support staff is to provide ARS researchers with the ability to achieve their research goals. Our recommendation in regards to sharing best practices does not envision changing this role for animal care staff. However, when animal care or veterinary support staff members wish to display initiative in developing animal care techniques which can enhance animal welfare, such as improved animal enrichment processes, they should be encouraged in their efforts, and appropriately recognized. This includes considering animal care activities that promote animal welfare in performance evaluations and, when appropriate, allowing animal care staff and research technicians to act as co-authors or lead authors on scientific publications.

Broadly speaking, substantial components of the panel's recommendations for improvements in the ARS animal care programs focused on enhanced training of IACUC members and animal care staff and additional opportunities to disseminate best animal care practices. Traditional methods of helping to meet these recommendations would involve travel of ARS individuals to training seminars or scientific conferences. Several ARS individuals noted the difficulty in complying with these recommendations due to travel caps within the federal government. The panel is very careful about prescribing specific steps in the efforts of ARS to meet the panel's recommendations. However, in this case one suggestion may be to exempt travel associated with efforts to improve animal welfare from the existing travel caps. Such an action would communicate to ARS employees the importance the agency assigns to promoting animal welfare while simultaneously signaling to the general public that animal welfare is a priority.

CONCLUSION

The Agricultural Research Service - Animal Handling and Welfare Panel visited 5 ARS research sites: The Livestock and Range Research Laboratory at Miles City, Montana; the Livestock Behavioral Research Unit in West Lafayette, Indiana; the Southeast Poultry Research Laboratory, in Athens, Georgia; the Richard B. Russell Agricultural Research Center in Athens, Georgia; and the National Animal Disease Center in Ames, Iowa. Based upon the observations of the panel members *no evidence* of poor animal handling, animal abuse, or inadequate veterinary care was observed or identified. Furthermore, the facilities were found to be in compliance with ARS Policies and Procedures, particularly in regards to the composition and function of the local animal care oversight committees, although operations of the IACUC varied between facilities. The panel has provided recommendations and refinements specific to each site to improve compliance with both the letter and spirit of ARS Policies and Procedures in regards to animal welfare and oversight. Additionally, the panel has provided recommendations which we believe will encourage improvements in the overall animal care and oversight programs operated within ARS.

APPENDIX A – SUMMARY OF PUBLIC COMMENT

The open comment period was held between June 29, 2015, and July 14, 2015. Written comments were submitted to a specific email box or the REE Advisory Board Office. A total of six written comments were received during this time frame. At the public meeting on March 18, 2015, verbal comments were received from three organizations. Below is a summary of the public comments received:

Written Comments

- Six written comments were received.
- One commenter clarified that the National Animal Disease Center currently has an assurance with the National Institutes of Health, Office of Laboratory Animal Welfare (OLAW).
- Five commenters encouraged the panel to add additional information and clarification on how the locations were selected by the panel and the methodology for the site reviews.
- Four commenters encouraged ARS to comply with the Animal Welfare Act, register every ARS animal research facility with the Animal and Plant Health Inspection Service (APHIS), and seek APHIS inspections of all animal facilities.
- Three commenters suggested that ARS should more fully utilize the National Agricultural Library's Animal Welfare Information Center.
- One commenter suggested that ARS should standardize the operation of the IACUCs, update the ARS Strategic Plan to include references to animal care and well-being, and utilize additional measures to upgrade facilities and facility management plans.
- One commenter suggested that ARS should formulate and disseminate new policies and procedures on animal welfare and train employees on the new policies and procedures.
- One commenter suggested that each IACUC should have two non-affiliated members on the IACUC; one of these non-affiliated members should be a bio-ethicist.
- One commenter was complimentary of the development and implementation of the ARS Animal Welfare Action Plan.

Verbal Comments

- A total of three verbal comments were received.
- All three commenters suggested adding additional information and clarification on how the locations were selected by the panel and the methodology for the site reviews.
- The commenters agreed with the findings and recommendations and encouraged ARS to harmonize and standardize the IACUCs across all ARS locations.

- One commenter praised ARS for the development and implementation of the Animal Welfare Action Plan.
- One commenter suggested that ARS should more fully utilize the National Agricultural Library's Animal Welfare Information Center.

In conclusion, the independent panel made the following edits to the report based on the comments received:

- Added information to the section on the Strengths of the Animal Care Program at the National Animal Disease Center indicating that the Center currently has an assurance with the National Institutes of Health, Office of Laboratory Animal Welfare (OLAW).
- Added a section on methodology, including information on how the locations were selected and how the site visits were conducted.

In: The Animal Welfare Act and Farm Animal ... ISBN: 978-1-63484-380-5
Editor: Albert V. Griffin

Chapter 5

ARS: U.S. MEAT ANIMAL RESEARCH CENTER REVIEW: INTERIM REPORT*

Gil H. Harden

United States Department of Agriculture Office of Inspector General
Washington, D.C. 20250

DATE:	
AUDIT NUMBER:	02007-0001-31 (1)
TO:	Chavonda Jacobs-Young Administrator Agricultural Research Service
ATTN:	Sharon Drumm Chief of Staff Administrator's Office
FROM:	Gil H. Harden Assistant Inspector General for Audit
SUBJECT:	ARS: U.S. Meat Animal Research Center Review – Interim Report

* This is an edited, reformatted and augmented version of report issued by the United States Department of Agriculture, Office of Inspector General, September 28, 2015.

The Agricultural Research Service (ARS) is the U.S. Department of Agriculture's (USDA) principal in-house research agency. The U.S. Meat Animal Research Center (USMARC), located in Clay Center, Nebraska, is an ARS research facility operated in collaboration with the University of Nebraska-Lincoln (UNL). USMARC's mission is to develop scientific information and new technology to solve high priority problems on beef, sheep, and swine.

On January 19, 2015, *The New York Times* published an article titled "U.S. Research Lab Lets Livestock Suffer in Quest for Profit." The article contains a number of statements regarding animal care and animal mortality levels at USMARC. Following the publication of the article, the USDA Office of Inspector General (OIG) received requests to examine the specific allegations made in the article and related conditions and procedures in place at USMARC.

OIG began its review on March 10, 2015, of USMARC's research practices and operations in response to concerns expressed by Congress and reported by the media regarding animal welfare. As our work continues, we will examine ARS' oversight and monitoring of USMARC, including how it relates to animal welfare. This Interim Report is intended to update you and Congressional requesters on our progress and initial observations on work completed to date.

Based on our review of *The New York Times* article and subsequent documentation obtained from ARS personnel, we identified 33 statements from the article to evaluate and attempt to determine their veracity. We have since performed fieldwork at USMARC; reviewed available ARS and UNL documentation dating back to 1983; interviewed key individuals, including over 30 current and former ARS and UNL personnel, and members of the Secretary's review panel; and researched meat industry and agricultural research statistics and norms. Given the sensitive nature of this review, we are providing information on the current status of our fieldwork. This information provides additional context to the statements made in *The New York Times* article.

To date, we have made significant progress towards the completion of our fieldwork on a majority of the 33 statements. However, the information presented in Exhibit A is subject to change, as we have not yet finalized our work on any of the 33 statements. Our preliminary observations are contained in Exhibit A of this document. At this time, we have not obtained comments on our preliminary observations from *The New York Times* reporter or the primary complainant, although we plan on contacting them to provide them the opportunity to provide additional information. At the completion of our fieldwork, we will issue a final report detailing the results of our review, including any findings, conclusions, and recommendations.

We conducted this performance audit in accordance with generally accepted government auditing standards. Those standards require that we plan and perform the audit to obtain sufficient, appropriate evidence to provide a reasonable basis for our findings and conclusions based on our audit objectives. We believe that the evidence obtained provides a reasonable basis for our findings and conclusions based on our audit objectives.

Exhibit A: Status of Fieldwork on Selected Items

After reviewing *The New York Times* article titled "U.S. Research Lab Lets Livestock Suffer in Quest for Profit," published January 19, 2015, we selected 33 specific statements to evaluate in an attempt to determine the veracity of the statements. The following is a listing of these 33 statements and a brief discussion of the current status of our evaluation of each statement. The status reflects our observations to date. These observations may be modified, as warranted, based on the remaining fieldwork to be performed to satisfy our audit objectives.

For reference, here is a link to *The New York Times* article: http://www.nytimes.com/2015/01/20/dining/animal-welfare-at-risk-in-experiments-for-meatindustry.html

Statement Number	Article Statement	Current Status of Fieldwork
1	"At a remote research center on the Nebraska plains, scientists are using surgery and breeding techniques to re-engineer the farm animal to fit the needs of the 21st-century meat industry."	Through a review of USMARC documents, we have determined that surgery and breeding have been used as part of the research performed at USMARC.
2	"Pigs are having many more piglets — up to 14, instead of the usual eight — but hundreds of those newborns, too frail or	Per the *2014 U.S. Pork Industry Productivity Analysis,* issued by the National Pork Board, the average number of piglets in a litter is around 13. After reviewing USMARC data

Statement Number	Article Statement	Current Status of Fieldwork
	crowded to move, are being crushed each year when their mothers roll over."	and documents, we determined that the average number of piglets per litter at USMARC since 1985 has been approximately 11. We determined that the prevalence of lightweight piglets at USMARC is in line with industry norms.[1] Through a review of USMARC data, we determined that hundreds of piglets die each year as a result of being crushed by their mothers. Through our research, we determined that this is one of the most common causes of preweaning piglet mortality in the pork industry. We determined that USMARC's live birth preweaning mortality rates were in line with industry norms.[2]
3	"Cows, which normally bear one calf at a time, have been retooled to have twins and triplets, which often emerge weakened or deformed, dying in such numbers that even meat producers have been repulsed."	We have no observations on this statement at this time.
4	"Last Mother's Day, at the height of the birthing season, two veterinarians struggled to sort through the weekend's toll: 25 rag-doll bodies. Five, abandoned by overtaxed mothers, had empty stomachs. Six had signs of pneumonia. Five had been savaged by coyotes."	Through a review of USMARC data, we have determined that a total of 25 sheep died on May 10 and 11, 2014. Of these sheep, five were coded as having died as a result of "starvation-empty stomach"[3] and another five were coded as having died as a result of a "predator strike." To date, we have not found evidence clearly supporting that six of the sheep had signs of pneumonia.

Statement Number	Article Statement	Current Status of Fieldwork
5	"... to be dumped in a vast excavation called the dead pit."	During our tour of the USMARC facility, we observed the "dead pit." We estimate the "dead pit" to be a trench measuring approximately 2 feet wide, 10 feet long, and at least 15 feet deep. Animal remains are placed in the trench and immediately covered with dirt. Based on research into agricultural practices, we determined that the burial of animal remains, particularly sheep remains, is a common and legal practice in agriculture.
6	"Little known outside the world of big agriculture, the center has one overarching mission: helping producers of beef, pork and lamb turn a higher profit as diets shift toward poultry, fish, and produce."	The stated mission of USMARC is "to develop scientific information and new technology to solve high priority problems on beef, sheep and swine."[4]
7	"The research to increase pig litters began in 1986;"	By reviewing USMARC documentation, we determined that research into pig litter size at USMARC began in 1986. We determined that the live birth preweaning mortality rates for the two populations associated with this research were generally in line with industry norms.[5]
8	"... center scientists have been operating on pigs' ovaries and brains in an attempt to make the sows more fertile."	Through a review of USMARC documentation and interviews of USMARC personnel, we determined that surgeries involving pigs' ovaries have been a part of USMARC's research. Our fieldwork found that surgeries performed in connection with research are focused on

Statement Number	Article Statement	Current Status of Fieldwork
		obtaining information on how various biological aspects interact and affect pig fertility, which, in turn, could be utilized by the industry in making selection[6] and management decisions. While surgery on pigs' brains was approved as part of a research plan at USMARC, we did not find any evidence that such surgery was actually performed at the facility.
9	"Of the 580,000 animals the center has housed since 1985, when its most ambitious projects got underway, at least 6,500 have starved."	Through a review of USMARC data, we determined that over 6,500 animals have been coded as having died due to starvation since 1985. Based on interviews of current and former USMARC personnel, the starvation code within the USMARC data does not indicate that animals were not provided adequate food by USMARC personnel. They explained that this code is used when an animal is found dead with no fat on its body. These deaths generally occur early in life as a result of complications with nursing.
10	"A single, treatable malady — mastitis, a painful infection of the udder — has killed more than 625."	We have no observations on this statement at this time.
11	"The center added a daring twist: pasture lambing, an attempt to take domesticated sheep, which are dependent on human help, and create a breed that can survive on its own."	We have reviewed USMARC documentation and performed extensive research into the sheep industry. We have found that pasture lambing is a common management practice in the United States that has been utilized by producers for a number of years.[7] Additionally, researchers outside of USMARC

Statement Number	Article Statement	Current Status of Fieldwork
		have studied pasture lambing prior to the commencement of the research at USMARC.[8]
12	"They withheld help for the newborns, typically leaving them in the pastures — till death, if necessary — to test whether mothers would respond to the young ones' growing desperation. "Cristiano Bouéres, a visiting student from Brazil, was assigned in 2012 to gather the dead lambs as part of his veterinary program at the university, and told to ignore the rest. "'Some days, 30 to 40 percent of the lambs were dead, and some of those still alive were in bad condition, separated from the moms, and they would be dead the next morning,' he said, dismayed and bewildered by the gulf between the experiment and his training. 'As a vet, you always appreciate animal welfare, and you want to have all of your patients taken care of and looking good and being fed.'" [....] "In a 2011 memo, the experiment's lead scientist, Kreg A. Leymaster, beseeched the center's director for help after 12	We have no observations on this statement at this time.

Statement Number	Article Statement	Current Status of Fieldwork
	lambs were killed in four days. The center added more guard dogs, but in just the first half of 2014, records show, 21 lambs were killed."	
13	"Out in the fields, the hailstorm sent the next day's body count soaring to 110. Death rates in the past three years have ranged between about one-quarter and one-third of the lambs, far beyond the 10 percent that many industry experts say is considered acceptable in sheep farming."	We have no observations on this statement at this time.
14	"Months into his new job at the center in 1989, Dr. Keen said, he got a call from a fellow worker asking him to help with a 'downed cow.' "There was a young cow, a teenager, with as many as six bulls," he recalled. "The bulls were being studied for their sexual libido, and normally you would do that by putting a single bull in with a cow for 15 minutes. But these bulls had been in there for hours mounting her. "The cow's head was locked in a cagelike device to keep her immobile, he said. 'Her back legs were broken. Her body was just	We have no observations on this statement at this time.

Statement Number	Article Statement	Current Status of Fieldwork
	torn up.' "Dr. Keen wanted to euthanize the animal, but the scientist in charge could not be tracked down for permission. A few hours later, the cow died."	
15	"A year before Dr. Keen encountered the dying cow, Robert A. Downey, executive director of the Capital Humane Society, in Lincoln, Neb., alerted by the staff, complained to the center director. 'Experimental surgery is being performed in some (not all) cases by untrained, unskilled and unsupervised staff,' Mr. Downey wrote. 'This has resulted in the suffering of animals and in some cases the subsequent death of animals.'"	We have no observations on this statement at this time.
16	"During a visit, he said, he saw animals headed to surgery that fell from carts or were pushed to the floor by their handlers,"	We have no observations on this statement at this time.
17	"The center does not have the veterinarians to be present during experiments, even if it wanted them to. Twenty years ago, it employed six scientists with veterinary degrees..."	We have interviewed current and former ARS officials. We have found that USMARC previously employed a number of scientists who also possessed veterinary degrees. A scientist's primary responsibility is to conduct research, and thus would be present at any experiments they conducted, whether they have a

Statement Number	Article Statement	Current Status of Fieldwork
		veterinary degree or not. All scientists, regardless of whether or not they have a veterinary degree, have the same animal care responsibilities.[9] The primary responsibility for animal care falls to the Veterinary Medical Officer (VMO), who attends some surgeries (and has the right to attend/participate in any and all surgeries or other procedures) and reviews health records to ensure the proper care of animals, including animals on which surgery was performed. The VMO receives assistance from an experienced veterinary technician, along with faculty and students from the Great Plains Veterinary Education Center, which includes four additional veterinarians. USMARC has unsuccessfully attempted to hire scientists who are also Doctors of Veterinary Medicine.
18	"That veterinarian, Shuna A. Jones, wrote to scientists and managers in 2011 and 2012 with a variety of concerns, including barns so stuffed with pigs that workers could not clean them, resulting in spates of diarrhea and respiratory disease. 'This is a scheduling nightmare,' wrote Dr. Jones, who declined to be interviewed. 'We have pigs everywhere.'"	Through a review of USMARC data and interviews of USMARC personnel, we determined that this email stemmed from USMARC changing its farrowing system. For a brief period during the transition, the two farrowing systems overlapped and created a hectic situation. Our review of USMARC's swine health data did not find evidence that there was a marked increase in diarrhea or respiratory diseases during this period. Furthermore, we determined that the live birth piglet mortality rates for this period were within

Statement Number	Article Statement	Current Status of Fieldwork
		industry norms.[10]
19	"Thirty to 40 have died on average each year of exposure to bad weather, records show — not including storms in which hundreds have perished, center scientists say."	Through a review of USMARC data, we determined that, on average, approximately 43 cattle have died annually due to exposure, including those that died in storms. We determined that the cattle deaths as a result of exposure to weather from 1985 to 2014 are generally in line with industry norms.[11]
20	"Dr. Keen, who now works for the University of Nebraska- Lincoln, said he and his students were startled last March to come across an emaciated ewe, in plain view of center employees, unable to eat because of a jaw abscess that had likely been growing for months. The ewe eventually died..."	We have no observations on this statement at this time.
21	"...becoming the 245th animal to succumb to an abscess since 1985."	We have reviewed USMARC data. We found that more than 245 animals have died at USMARC from abscesses since 1985. The 30-year mortality rate specifically related to abscesses was about 0.006, 0.042, and 0.081 percent in cattle, swine, and sheep, respectively.[12]
22	"Visiting the center in the late 1980s, the renowned animal welfare expert Temple Grandin approached a herd of cows. They panicked. 'When cattle run away, that's indicative of rough	After reviewing Ms. Grandin's report to USMARC, we determined that Ms. Grandin stated that the behavior of some cattle that she observed at one particular building at the facility may indicate rough handling. She also wrote that she had heard of instances of rough handling or yelling by

Statement Number	Article Statement	Current Status of Fieldwork
	handling, screaming and yelling,' said Ms. Grandin, who gave the center a report suggesting ways to treat cattle more humanely."	certain employees, though she acknowledges that she could not verify whether these accusations were true. In her report, Ms. Grandin also noted good cattle handling and employee behavior that she observed at numerous buildings. Furthermore, we spoke to cattle consultants that have visited USMARC in recent years and all of them stated that they had never observed any mistreatment of animals at the facility.
23	"Roger Ellis, a scientist and veterinarian who now works for a cattle nutrition company, said that when he determined about 10 years ago that a sheep had died at least in part from neglect, a center official pressed him to 'soften the diagnosis.' Dr. Ellis said that he refused, and that the center had an outside veterinarian change the death record."	We have no observations on this statement at this time.
24	"An animal manager, Devin M. Gandy, complained in 2012 that swine were kept in pens so small, 4 feet by 4 feet, that they appeared to violate basic rules on animal care."	Through a review of USMARC documentation and interviews of USMARC personnel, we determined that an email was written expressing concerns about pen sizes and that a USMARC scientist responded with a comment about "a lot of time being wasted addressing a non-issue." As indicated by the email chain and our own interviews, the [redacted] looked into the situation and concluded everything

Statement Number	Article Statement	Current Status of Fieldwork
		was in order. Furthermore, within the same email chain, the individual was praised by the USMARC [redacted] for having brought the issue to everyone's attention; the [redacted] stated that animal welfare issues will never be considered a "waste of time." Based on our review of the description of the circumstances, it appears that the pen size did, in fact, meet the space recommendations contained in the 1988 Guide for the Care and Use of Agricultural Animals in Agricultural Research and Teaching.[13,14]
25	"Geoffrey Hirsch, a former technician, recalled helping with a routine procedure about 12 years ago to extract lung tissue from the carcass of a young pig. But efforts to euthanize the pig had failed, he said; it was still thrashing and gagging. Worse, Mr. Hirsch said, the scientist who had erred 'seemed to be getting some kind of enjoyment out of this thing, talking and shouting at the animal," 'How do you like that, pig?' Stuff like that. The whole process was shocking." The scientist leading the trial stormed back to his office to write a complaint about the animal's treatment, after informing	We have no observations on this statement at this time.

Statement Number	Article Statement	Current Status of Fieldwork
	his boss, William Laegreid. 'There were ill feelings towards him and me and the unit after that,' recalled Dr. Laegreid, who now directs the veterinary science program at the University of Wyoming."	
26	"As for Dr. Keen, his attempts to raise alarms culminated in May..."	We have no observations on this statement at this time.
27	"Yet unsettling side effects surfaced. Some 95 percent of the females born with male siblings had deformed vaginas."	Through interviews of multiple veterinarians and our own research, we determined that the deformity referenced by the article is called "freemartinism."[15] We determined that it is a very commonly known condition that results from a male/female twin set, rather than a unique side effect that arose as a result of the Twinning Project. Furthermore, multiple veterinarians have confirmed that, other than being sterile, animals with this condition suffer no ill effects or pain and can still enter the food supply.
28	"When the Twinning Project's lead scientist retired in 2013, no one stepped up to succeed him. The surviving cows were sold, though the center is still trying with little success to sell the bulls' semen."	We have interviewed USMARC officials and reviewed USMARC data and documentation. We found that USMARC began dispersing its twinning herd before the Twinning Project's lead scientist retired. USMARC has only actively attempted to sell its Twinning Project's bull semen once, in a 3-day online auction, and was able to sell over 40 percent of the semen lots offered for sale.

Statement Number	Article Statement	Current Status of Fieldwork
29	"...the Agriculture Department requires that the center do what many universities and companies do: appoint a review committee that holds regular meetings, keeps minutes and approves or rejects each experiment after carefully evaluating animal safety."	We have reviewed ARS Directives and USMARC documentation and interviewed USMARC officials. We found that USMARC is required to appoint an Institutional Animal Care and Use Committee (IACUC) that holds meetings, keeps minutes of meetings, and approves or disapproves proposed experiments that involve animal subjects.[16] In February 2015, the Secretary of Agriculture appointed an Agricultural Research Service Animal Handling and Welfare Review Panel (ARS-AHWRP) to review animal care and well-being policies, procedures, and standards. On March 30, 2015, the ARS-AHWRP reported that it found the IACUC at USMARC was not adequately fulfilling its intended role.
30	"However, Gene White, a retired university veterinarian and scientist who sits on its animal care committee, said the change occurred because the school was seeking accreditation, which imposes stringent requirements. "'We had to have more control over the animals out there, which was not acceptable to the U.S.D.A,' Dr. White said."	Through interviews of UNL and USMARC personnel, we determined that personnel at UNL did not believe the transfer of ownership was an effort by USMARC to avoid the additional oversight that would result from UNL seeking accreditation. The change in ownership was reportedly made as a result of financial considerations between UNL and USMARC. Furthermore, the accreditation that UNL sought, and has since received, required a site visit to all facilities providing care to animals owned by the University. The transfer did not result in USMARC being exempt from receiving a site visit from the accrediting organization, since UNL

Statement Number	Article Statement	Current Status of Fieldwork
		still owned some cattle located at USMARC after the transfer. The accrediting organization did not identify any significant issues regarding animal welfare at USMARC during its site visit to the facility.
31	"Last year, the center set out to show that its cows could thrive on a growth stimulant called Zilmax. Months earlier, the drug had been withdrawn by its manufacturer, Merck & Company, amid concern in the meat industry that it caused rare complications, like hooves that slough off, and was associated with higher death rates."	Through a review of USMARC documentation and our own research, we determined that Zilmax[17] was withdrawn from the market in August 2013.[18] We determined that while USMARC has conducted research involving Zilmax since the drug was removed from the market, none of these experiments included an objective to prove that cows could thrive on the stimulant.[19]
32	"Last February, Katherine Whitman, a University of Nebraska veterinarian who works at the center, proposed an experiment to find more effective pain medicine for two common procedures on sheep: tail removal and castration."	Through a review of USMARC documentation and interviews of USMARC personnel, we determined that a proposal was submitted for the experiment described in the article, and that proposal was turned down by a USMARC scientist because it did not fall into one of the two approved objectives for sheep research at USMARC.[20] All research at USMARC is required to meet approved research objectives in order for appropriated money to be expended on it. Accordingly, as the research proposed did not relate to either of the approved research objectives for sheep, the research project was not approved.

Statement Number	Article Statement	Current Status of Fieldwork
33	"Another reason for the denial: The center said it lacked the expertise to assess the pain felt by animals."	Through a review of ARS' responses to the article's author's inquiries, we found that USMARC stated that it lacked the necessary expertise to perform the proposed research because it did not have any animal behaviorists, stress physiologists, or other experts on staff that would be required to collect the necessary information. During our interviews at USMARC, USMARC staff stated they are able to tell if an animal is in pain, but they do not have the expertise necessary to objectively measure pain in a manner that would have allowed such research to pass a peer review.[21] Through a review of USMARC documentation, we determined that USMARC does not have any animal behaviorist or stress physiologist positions.

End Notes

1 Per nationalhogfarmer.com, pigs born weighing less than 2.2 pounds are considered lightweight. Lightweight births usually account for approximately 15 percent of pig births within the pork industry. From 1985 to 2014, lightweight pigs accounted for approximately 14.8 percent of pig births at USMARC.

2 Live birth preweaning mortality refers to piglets that were born alive (i.e., not stillborn) and died prior to weaning. To calculate the live birth preweaning mortality rate, the number of live born pigs that died prior to weaning is divided by the total number of live born pigs. The National Pork Board's 2014 U.S. Pork Industry Productivity Analysis contains average preweaning mortality rates and associated standard deviations from 2008 through 2013. We considered any rate falling within one standard deviation of the quoted rates to be within industry norms. From 2008 through 2013, all of USMARC's live birth preweaning mortality rates fell within one standard deviation of the rates contained in the National Pork Board's analysis for those years.

3 Based on interviews of current and former USMARC personnel, the starvation code within the USMARC data does not indicate that animals were not provided adequate food by USMARC personnel. They explained that this code is used when an animal is found dead

with no fat on its body. These deaths generally occur early in life as a result of complications with nursing.

[4] The Roman L. Hruska U.S. Meat Animal Research Center, obtained on February 20, 2015.

[5] For the definition, calculation, and source for industry norms related to live birth preweaning mortality, see Footnote 2. From 2008 through 2013, USMARC's live birth preweaning mortality rates for the two primary populations related to the facility's pig litter size research fell within one standard deviation of the rates contained in the National Pork Board's analysis for 4 of those 6 years. For the other two years, USMARC's rate was slightly below industry norms one year and was slightly above in the other year.

[6] Selection refers to the action of a breeder in selecting individual animals from which to breed, in order to obtain some desired quality or characteristic in the descendants.

[7] An Animal and Plant Health Inspection Service study on lambing management practices in 2011 found that 69.4 percent of lambs born in the western United States, 59.4 percent of lambs born in the central United States, and 23.6 percent of lambs born in the eastern United States were born using a pasture lambing management system.

[8] For example, "Lambing Ewes Outside as an Integral Part of Low Input Sheep Production in the Mid-Appalachian Region," Animal Sciences Research and Reviews, Special Circular 156. The Ohio State University. Accessed at <http://ohioline.osu.edu/sc156/sc156_44.html> on March 30, 2015.

[9] Per ARS Directive 635.1, all research scientists are to ensure that they personally, their technicians, caretakers, students, and others follow regulations and standards for humane care of animals used in any manner by them and/or their subordinates.

[10] See Footnote 2.

[11] According to an Animal and Plant Health Inspection Service's report titled Cattle and Calves Nonpredator Death Loss in the United States, 2010, weather related deaths in beef operations accounted for up to approximately 15 percent and 22 percent of nonpredator deaths in cattle and calves, respectively. From 1985 to 2014, weather related deaths have accounted for approximately 10 percent of nonpredator deaths of all live born cattle (i.e., cattle and calves) at USMARC.

[12] To calculate the mortality rate, we divided the total number of abscess-related deaths in a species since 1985 by the total population of animals in that species that have been housed at USMARC since 1985. If an animal was housed at USMARC multiple years since 1985, it was counted as an individual animal each of those years because the animal had the opportunity to die from abscess(es) each year (i.e., if an animal was housed at USMARC for five years, it would be counted in the total population five times for this calculation).

[13] Published by Consortium for Developing a Guide for the Care and Use of Agricultural Animals in Agricultural Research and Teaching, March 1988.

[14] The most current version of this document is dated January 2010. We noted that the minimum floor area recommendation for adult swine in the current version matches the recommendation in the March 1988 version.

[15] Freemartinism is one of the most commonly found forms of intersexuality in cattle. A bovine freemartin is a sterile female calf, born with a male twin, that shows an underdeveloped or mis-developed genital tract due to the in utero passage of male hormones between the twins. The condition is found in over 90 percent of cattle from these types of pregnancies.

[16] ARS Directive 130.4, dated August 1, 2002.

[17] Zilmax is a beta-agonist, a class of growth promotants.

[18] The manufacturer cited the desire to study potential causes of lameness and other mobility issues.

[19] Experiment number 5438-31000-092-04 had an objective of to "determine if feeding [Zilmax] decreases or increases the energy requirements of finishing beef steers." Experiment number 5438-31000-092-07 had an objective of to "estimate the effects of open vs. shaded pens of cattle with and without [Zilmax] on heat stress, animal performance, and carcass characteristics."

[20] The two approved objectives related to sheep research at USMARC concerned 1) reducing the prevalence of ovine progressive pneumonia in sheep and 2) developing and evaluating an easy-care maternal line of prolific hair sheep.

[21] A peer review is a process through which an article containing scientific results is subjected to review by other scientists to ensure that it meets scientific standards before the article is accepted for publication in a scientific journal.

In: The Animal Welfare Act and Farm Animal ... ISBN: 978-1-63484-380-5
Editor: Albert V. Griffin

Chapter 6

ANIMAL WELFARE ACTION PLAN*

Agricultural Research Service

INTRODUCTION

The Agricultural Research Service's (ARS) Animal Welfare Action Plan contains three primary emphasis areas: policies and procedures, training, and oversight. While the health and wellbeing of the animals in the care of ARS and of all animals in the agricultural industry have always been of high significance to us, we are taking the events of recent months as an opportunity to further strengthen and then institutionalize a continuous improvement system for animal welfare in ARS. In the coming months and years, ARS animal handling policies and procedures will be updated, a new training program for all who come into contact with animals at work will be rolled out, and the establishment of an internal structure to increase coordination and oversight of animal research will be realized.

1. Policies and Procedures

ARS has two official Policies and Procedures (P&P), 635.1 and 130.4, that govern animal care and handling. Upon receipt of recommendations from

---

* This is an edited, reformatted and augmented version of a document issued by the United States Department of Agriculture, March 20, 2015 (updated June 17, 2015).

the external panel and deliberations from the internal ARS Animal Welfare Leadership Committee and Task Force, the two existing P&Ps will be consolidated, updated, and reissued. In addition, an implementation plan will be developed to lead ARS' path forward toward executing upgrades to the Animal Welfare Program.

1.1. Inputs to Formulate Policies and Procedures

USDA External Animal Handling and Welfare Review Panel (USMARC and ARS Review)

The Secretary of the United States Department of Agriculture (USDA) has appointed an external Animal Handling and Welfare Review Panel. The panel consists of animal research and welfare experts from land grant universities, and is charged with evaluating animal use, care, and wellbeing at the U.S. Meat Animal Research Center (USMARC), with a complete report by March 20, 2015. During the next six months, the panel will produce a recommended course of action to strengthen animal handling protocols, procedures, and practices across all ARS animal research facilities. This input will be used to formulate updated policies and procedures within ARS. The panel's operating charter is included in Appendix A.

USDA Office of the Inspector General Audit

The Office of the Inspector General is performing an audit with the objectives to review the research practices and operations of the USMARC to evaluate the concerns expressed by Congress and reported by the media regarding animal welfare. They will also examine ARS' oversight and monitoring of USMARC as it relates to animal welfare. Their audit results, anticipated January 2016, will also inform ARS policies and procedures going forward.

1.2. Animal Welfare Ombudsman

In addition to reinforcing the Whistleblower Protections available to all Federal employees, the updated ARS policies and procedures will include guidance on a new option to report findings to the Animal Welfare Ombudsman. The Animal Welfare Ombudsman provides confidential, impartial, and independent assistance to individuals and groups who have complaints or concerns related to animal welfare in ARS animal research facilities. The Ombudsman provides a safe and confidential forum for internal and external individuals or groups who work on ARS grounds to service complaints or concerns about animal welfare. The Ombudsman provides reports to the ARS Administrator on at least an annual basis including the number of complainants assisted, problem categories, issues and observations, trends, concerns, and recommendations. In addition to summarizing the results of the year's work, the annual report will alert the ARS leadership to problems and trends and help decision-making within ARS to foster a renewed culture of animal welfare.

On January 23, 2015, ARS Administrator Dr. Chavonda Jacobs-Young appointed Dr. Eileen Thacker the first Animal Welfare Ombudsman at ARS. Dr. Thacker is a veterinarian with a Ph.D. in pathology, and is currently the ARS National Program Leader for both Food Safety and Animal Health and is Board Certified in Veterinary Microbiology. The ARS Animal Welfare Ombudsman can be reached via email at animalwellbeing@ars.usda.gov, and encourages internal and external communications about ARS animal welfare concerns or complaints.

More information on the Animal Welfare Ombudsman program is found in Appendix C.

2. Training

The Animal Welfare Act (AWA) and the Public Health Service (PHS) Policy on Humane Care and Use of Laboratory Animals provide guidance and regulations to ensure that all animals used for research in the United States are treated in a humane manner. It has been the policy of ARS to follow all regulations of the AWA and PHS to ensure that the animals used in research by the Agency are treated appropriately and humanely. An integral part of both the AWA and the PHS guidelines is a comprehensive animal welfare training program. Therefore, the ARS Animal Welfare Training Program is designed to meet AWA and PHS requirements for basic and specialized training in the humane care and use of animals, and will train researchers, postdocs, or technicians who use or plan to use animals; Institutional Animal Care and Use Committee (IACUC) members; animal care staff; animal surgery staff; and management or administrative staff of animal handling facilities.

All such ARS employees need to receive training within the first 60 days of implementation of this plan or within the first 60 days of employment. Employees of locations co-located with Universities and receiving training associated with the University would be required to provide documentation of all training within the first 60 days of implementation. Completion of all training requirements listed is required within 12 months of the official announcement of this action plan.

More specific information on training, including sources and curriculum, is available in Appendix D. This training plan is implementation-ready, as it is an integral part of the ARS Animal Welfare Program moving forward.

3. Oversight

3.1. ARS Animal Care and Use Officer (ACUO)

ARS will establish a new Animal Care and Use Officer (ACUO) at Headquarters to lead the oversight to ensure all animal research locations are in compliance with ARS policies and procedures on animal welfare. The ACUO will be a professional with a DVM degree, and possibly a DVM-PhD, who is qualified to evaluate animal care, use, and well-being, as well as policies, procedures, and experimental plans and methods that may affect animals in research settings. The ACUO's primary responsibilities will include receiving and reviewing IACUC minutes from labs across ARS, overseeing training requirements, and reviewing or coordinating reviews of experimental protocols for animal research in ARS.

3.2. ARS Animal Welfare Leadership Committee and Task Force

ARS has established two bodies—the ARS Animal Welfare Leadership Committee and the Animal Welfare Task Force—to coordinate, review, and strengthen relevant ARS programs and offices with the aim of assisting Agency leadership in fulfilling its responsibilities to the animals under ARS care. This Leadership Committee is comprised of senior program and line managers in ARS and chaired by the Deputy Administrator for Animal Production and Protection, Office of National Programs. The Leadership Committee will provide guidance to the Animal Welfare Task Force, comprised of field and headquarter leaders, plus an animal welfare program leader from the Animal and Plant Health Inspection Service (APHIS). As recommended in the report *Critical Role of Animal Science Research in Food Security and Sustainability*[1], the Leadership Committee will also be tasked with ensuring the consideration of social and environmental aspects of animal research are included in the national program planning process. ARS will work with the National Academy of Sciences to address the recommendations of the report to more closely integrate socioeconomic and animal science research. The Task Force will also oversee, lead, and often participate in ARS animal welfare program inspections to identify gaps in current ARS animal care and use protocols and procedures and to develop implementation plans to address identified gaps.

Together, these groups working in concert with ACUO are charged with promoting and maintaining a vigilant, community-owned, animal welfare culture across ARS locations. More about the groups is available in Appendix B.

3.3. Accreditation and Inspection Pilot Program with APHIS

ARS intends to voluntarily register its animal research locations with APHIS. ARS is also exploring options to make an arrangement with APHIS Animal Welfare Inspectors for periodic review of ARS animal care and use at the various locations. Third party animal welfare accreditation is an option that may be feasible for some ARS locations. The ARS Animal Care and Use Officer will work closely with the Animal Welfare Task Force to provide resources and assistance to those ARS locations that will explore third party accreditation.

APHIS and ARS are also collaborating to develop a pilot project to assess the animal welfare standards, compliance monitoring, and Institutional Animal Care and Use Committee (IACUC) oversight of animals used at specific ARS research facilities. The results of the pilot project will be carefully evaluated and next steps formulated. ARS and APHIS will develop a formal partnership and program that will ensure ARS facilities maintain consistent practices for adhering to all necessary animal welfare standards, including those outlined in APHIS' animal welfare regulations. Key steps being planned include:

- APHIS will review existing ARS animal welfare and IACUC oversight and guidelines for its animals used in research.
- APHIS will evaluate the application of the guidelines at selected ARS facilities to establish baseline compliance measurements.
- APHIS will work with ARS to develop inspection procedures, checklists, results reporting mechanisms, and other necessary supporting documentation for the pilot inspection program.
- APHIS and ARS will conduct pilot facility inspections.
- ARS will review results and develop a formal partnership and facility inspection program.

4. Animal Welfare Program Implementation Timeline

ARS is fully aware that without its research animals, ARS' vital studies on animal and human health and food safety would not be possible. The implementation roadmap identifies specific steps and milestones to continuously improve ARS' management and research practices and reaffirm its commitment to meet the highest standards of animal use, care, and well-being. The following table summarizes the implementation roadmap.

Dates	Milestones/Deliverables	Notes
01/2015	Established an Animal Welfare (AW) email portal.	Established animalwellbeing@ars.usda.gov to encourage internal and external communications about ARS animal welfare concerns.
01/2015	Appointed an Animal Welfare Ombudsman.	Dr. Eileen Thacker, a veterinarian with a Ph.D. in pathology, was appointed as ARS' first Animal Welfare Ombudsman on January 23, 2015.
01/2015	Established an Animal Welfare Leadership Committee.	Leveraged and expanded the ARS Biosafety, Safety and Health Leadership Steering Committee to include animal welfare. The committee is chaired by Dr. Steve Kappes.
01/2015	Analyzed existing Animal Welfare training programs.	Evaluated and analyzed existing Animal Welfare training programs across ARS locations.
02/2015	Formed an external review panel.	An Animal Handling and Welfare Review Panel (AHWRP) was formed with experts from land grant universities.
02/2015	Conducted external panel review of USMARC Animal Welfare program.	The AHWRP started their review on February 24 and provided its initial findings to the Secretary on March 9. A finalized report incorporating NAREEE board comments was due by April 2015. The Secretary received these comments on April 30, 2015.
02/2015	Established an Animal Welfare Task Force.	Dr. Don Lay with 6 ARS and APHIS subject matter experts chairs the Task Force.

Dates	Milestones/Deliverables	Notes
03/2015	Update ARS Animal Welfare policies & procedures.	Began updating ARS Policies and Procedures No. 635.1 – Humane Animal Care and Use. Began updating ARS Policies and Procedures No. 130.4 – Animal Care and Use Committee. These will be updated based on the recommendations provided by the independent panel review during its second phase.
03/2015	Standardize agency-wide Animal Welfare training curriculum.	Leverage existing ARS training courses, APHIS courses, and third party training courses.
03/2015	Implement AHWRP's USMARC review recommendations.	The AHWRP provided its draft USMARC review report with seven recommendations: • Develop and implement written agreements with University of Nebraska Lincoln (UNL) and any other research or teaching partners. To be completed by July 2015. • Develop and implement an animal handling training and documentation program. Began training development in March 2015. On March 27, 2015, 64 ARS employees and 66 UNL employees completed training developed by UNL Attending Veterinarian Dr. Kelly Heath and his assistant, Kathy Pinkerton, based on the AHWRP recommendations. • Extend the electronic medical records database to include all species housed at USMARC. The sheep database was implemented on April 1, 2015. The addition of sheep health records to the electronic database means that all animals at USMARC are now tracked in the database.

Dates	Milestones/Deliverables	Notes
		• Develop and implement processes that promote a robustly functioning IACUC with proper training. • A new IACUC composed of 11 members and 2 alternates was named on April 27, 2015. All members and alternates have completed required training. Training certifications are recorded via the American Association for Laboratory Animal Science (AALAS) online system. • Appropriate training for IACUC members on processes, requirements, and expectations. All members completed by April 16, 2015. • Properly convened meetings be held regularly, and that criteria be developed for what types of research proposals should receive additional review and discussion at IACUC meetings and those that may be appropriately reviewed by designated IACUC members outside of a convened meeting. Meetings held May 5 and May 14. Any research proposal that requires an animal to undergo major surgery (as defined by the Federation of Animal Science Societies' guidelines) or be euthanized must be reviewed during full committee meetings. • Development of a consistent IACUC review process that will review and evaluate the topics related to animal welfare as indicated by the Ag Guide. A Standard Operating Procedure has been developed for the IACUC review process and other IACUC activities. • All individuals associated with animal

Dates	Milestones/Deliverables	Notes
		care or research receive training on the role and importance of the IACUC in animal welfare and oversight. Kelly Heath, UNL Attending Veterinarian, provided General Regulations Training to all individuals associated with animal care. • IACUC members should inspect all areas where animals are held, handled or used, even if animals are not present at the time of inspection. The IACUC SOP (standard operating procedures) addresses facility inspections. • Reviews of proposed research or facility inspections should not be conducted unless a properly constituted IACUC is in place. The IACUC has been properly reconstituted; the reconstituted IACUC met for the first time on May 5, 2015, to review a set of the most time-sensitive research protocols. • Attending Veterinarian should not serve as the chair of the USMARC IACUC. A new panel chair has been appointed. USMARC research physiologist Jeff Vallet, who is not the USMARC attending veterinarian, has assumed the role of Chair of the IACUC. Completed as of March 13, 2015. • Use of all vertebrate animals at USMARC should be reviewed and approved by the IACUC. Completed as of March 13, 2015.
04/2015	Begin progress reporting.	Monthly report on the implementation of AHWRP recommendations.
04/2015	Enhance pasture lambing and calving	Review and enhance USMARC pasture lambing and calving.

Dates	Milestones/Deliverables	Notes
	protocol.	
04/2015	Conduct external panel review of ARS Animal Welfare programs.	The AHWRP will start its review in April and report to the Undersecretary in August 2015.
05/2015	Conduct ARS' internal Animal Welfare program inspections.	Ongoing assessment to continuously improve the effectiveness of Animal Welfare programs through assessments and evaluations.
06/2015	Implement recommendations from internal Animal Welfare program inspections.	Continuous improvement of Animal Welfare programs.
06/2015	Begin agency-wide training.	Ongoing Animal Welfare training based on the training plan defined.
06/2015	Voluntarily apply for APHIS registration.	Register ARS animal research facilities with APHIS. Complete the registration of ARS animal research facilities in 18 months.
06/2015	Begin ARS and APHIS Collaborative Pilot Project.	Begin APHIS Animal Care and ARS collaboration to establish baseline measures, resources, and operational requirements.
07/2015	Establish an Animal Care and Use Officer (ACUO).	The ACUO would be a GS-15 professional with a DVM or DVM-PhD degree at the Headquarters.
10/2015	Implement AHWRP's ARS Agency-wide review recommendations.	Periodically review Animal Welfare practices and ensure that Animal Welfare is incorporated as an Agency value at all levels.
12/2015	Begin accreditation and certification.	Work with associations and industry to begin certifying ARS laboratory animal research facilities. Complete the accreditation of all ARS laboratory animal research facilities in 5 years.

Appendix A – Animal Handling and Welfare Review Panel Charter

Independent External Panel Review

An external Animal Handling and Welfare Review Panel (AHWRP) has been appointed by the Secretary of the United States Department of Agriculture (USDA) under the authority of section 1409 A(e) of the National Agricultural Research, Extension, and Teaching Policy Act. The panel consists of animal research and welfare experts from land grant universities. The panel has been charged with evaluating animal use, care, and well-being at the U.S. Meat Animal Research Center (USMARC), with a complete report within 60 days. During the next six months, the panel will produce a recommended course of action to strengthen animal handling protocols, procedures, and practices across all ARS animal research facilities.

1.1. Panel Operating Charter

The objective of the AHWRP is to review ARS agency-wide animal care, use, and well-being policies, procedures, standards, and practices. The AHWRP will begin with an immediate review of USMARC and subsequently expand to review several other ARS animal research facilities. The AHWRP will report its findings and recommendations to the Secretary of USDA and the Undersecretary of Research, Education, and Economics (REE). The panel was charged with conducting an open, transparent, and independent review. The AHWRP review will be carried out in two phases. For the first phase, the panel was tasked to:

- Review ARS/REE/USDA Policies and Procedures (P&Ps) providing requirements and guidance for care, use, and well-being of animals used in research.
- Visit USMARC at Clay Center, Nebraska.
- Inspect facilities, pens, fields, etc., where animals are housed or involved in experimentation.
- Review the composition of the location's Institutional Animal Care and Use Committee (IACUC), records of its meetings, and evidence of compliance with agency P&Ps.
- Review processes used to select topics, and evaluate experimental designs and protocols under the IACUC.

- Assess care and well-being training needs for staff having responsibility for handling animals.

This was accomplished by the following timeline:

- February 24-26, 2015 - The AHWRP members visited USMARC
- March 9, 2015 – Panel provided draft report of findings to the Secretary
- March 9, 2015 – Notice of public meeting published in the Federal Register with a link to the draft report; Secretary Vilsack orders ARS to take steps to begin the implementation of immediately actionable recommendations contained within the report
- March 9-18, 2015 – Public comment period
- March 18, 2015– Panel's public meeting (via teleconference) to present report and provide opportunity for oral comments
- March 18-23, 2015 – Panel updates report to address public comments
- March 23, 2015 – Panel provides report to National Agricultural Research, Education and Economics (NAREEE) Advisory Board
- March 30, 2015 - Notice of public meeting published in the Federal Register with the link to the updated report
- March 30-April 14, 2015 – NAREEE Board holds a second public comment period
- April 14, 2015 – NAREEE Board public meeting to discuss the final report with opportunity for verbal public comments
- April 14-21, 2015 – NAREEE Board finalized response and included public comments
- April 30, 2015 – NAREEE Board provided response to Secretary, Under Secretary, and ARS Administrator.

The AHWRP has completed its review of USMARC and prepared a report of its findings and recommendations to the USDA Secretary and the REE Under Secretary. The panel also met in a public forum to present its findings and recommendations and accept public input.

As a result of the discussion on April 14, 2015, the NAREEE Advisory Board identified the following recommendations to USDA:

- The USMARC and University of Nebraska Lincoln (UNL) agreements identified in Recommendation 1 of the Final Report from the ARS-AHWR Panel should also include clearly documented provisions on the appropriate animal handling and use policies and procedures.

- USDA should continue to ensure that the recommendations submitted by the ARSAHWR Panel are appropriately implemented at USMARC and continue to be followed, either through site visits or another appropriate agreement or mechanism.
- NAREEE supports the Secretary in requiring that the Institutional Animal Care and Use Committee (IACUC) must be properly constituted prior to any additional reviews or approvals of research protocols. Anything short of following *The Guide for the Care and Use of Agricultural Animals in Research and Teaching* (the Ag Guide, produced by the Federation of Animal Science Societies) is unacceptable. These standards are an appropriate and effective way to ensure animals are cared for and used appropriately in research protocols.

The second phase of the review will be completed in 180 days. The AHWRP will:

- Visit three to five ARS locations where livestock research is conducted.
- Inspect facilities, pens, fields, etc., where animals are housed or involved in experimentation.
- Review the composition of the location's IACUC, records of its meetings, and evidence of compliance with agency P&Ps.
- Review processes used to select topics, and evaluate experimental designs and protocols under the IACUC.
- Assess care and well-being training needs for staff having responsibility for handling animals.

Below is the projected timeline for the second phase:

- May 11 through June 30, 2015 – Panel will conduct site reviews and draft report
- July 6, 2015 – Provide draft report to the REE Under Secretary, publish report on website
- July 6-14, 2015 – Public Comment period and Public Meeting

- July 21, 2015 – Submit final report to REE Under Secretary, publish report on website
- July 21-August 19, 2015 – Public Comment period and Public Meeting, NAREEE Board comment period
- August 19, 2015 – NAREEE submits additional advice and recommendations to REE Under Secretary to finalize report

The panel is composed of five individuals who are experts in animal science research, veterinary medicine, and animal care from U.S. land grant universities. The panel is balanced in its membership in terms of points of view represented and the functions to be performed. One ex-officio member of the panel is the Chief Veterinary Officer of the Animal and Plant Health Inspection Service (APHIS). One member serves as the chairperson who leads the group in a fair and focused manner.

1.2. USMARC Review

The AHWRP members visited USMARC on February 24-26, 2015. They were given full access to the entire facility and inspected all animal housing sites and fields where animals were located and research activities that were underway. They observed animal handling and interviewed USMARC employees. They also reviewed processes for research and animal welfare oversight, the composition and function of the IACUC, on-site veterinary medical care, upkeep, maintenance, and regular review of animal facilities, and training of the Center's personnel.

The AHWRP has provided a draft USMARC review report to the Secretary and released the report for public review and comment on Monday, March 9, 2015. In late March 2015, the panel held a public hearing teleconference call to receive inputs and comments on the draft report from interested stakeholders. Public comments will be reviewed, and then the panel will finalize its report in April 2015. The AHWRP has made the following seven major recommendations:

- Develop and implement written agreements with University of Nebraska, Lincoln (UNL) and any other research or teaching partners. This draft document is under review by the UNL Office of General Counsel and USDA Office of General Counsel. We expect this to be finalized in late July 2015.
- Develop and implement an animal handling training and documentation program for all individuals involved with the handling

and use of animals in research. UNL Attending Veterinarian Dr. Kelly Heath and his assistant, Kathy Pinkerton developed training based on the initial Panel recommendations. On March 27, 2015, 64 ARS employees and 66 UNL employees completed the training. Dr. Heath certified completion for the participants. Appropriate information on how to report concerns was also provided and posted. The whistleblower policy is an aspect of the posted material.

- Extend the electronic medical records database to include all animal species housed at USMARC. The sheep health database was implemented on April 1, 2015. The addition of sheep health records to the electronic database means all animals at USMARC are now tracked in the database.
- Develop and implement processes that promote a robustly functioning IACUC with proper training. A new IACUC composed of 11 members and 2 alternates was named on April 27, 2015. All members and alternates have completed required training. Training certifications are recorded via the American Association for Laboratory Animal Science (AALAS) online system.
    - Appropriate training for IACUC members on processes, requirements, and expectations. All members completed by April 16, 2015.
    - Properly convened meetings be held regularly, and that criteria be developed for what types of research proposals should receive additional review and discussion at IACUC meetings and those that may be appropriately reviewed by designated IACUC members outside of a convened meeting. Meetings held May 5 and May 14. Any research proposal that requires an animal to undergo major surgery (as defined by the Federation of Animal Science Societies' guidelines) or be euthanized must be reviewed during full committee meetings.
    - Development of a consistent IACUC review process that will review and evaluate the topics related to animal welfare as indicated by the Ag Guide. A Standard Operating Procedure has been developed for the IACUC review process and other IACUC activities.
    - All individuals associated with animal care or research receive training on the role and importance of the IACUC in animal welfare and oversight. Dr. Kelly Heath, UNL Attending

Veterinarian, provided General Regulations Training to all individuals associated with animal care.

- IACUC members should inspect all areas where animals are held, handled or used, even if animals are not present at the time of inspection. The IACUC SOP (standard operating procedures) addresses facility inspections.

- *Reviews of proposed research or facility inspections should not be conducted unless a properly constituted IACUC is in place.* As outlined above, the IACUC processes have been revised, new committee membership has been appointed, and training for each member has been completed and certified by the AALAS. The revised IACUC process received REE approval, and is now fully functional and approved to renew research protocols and facility inspections. USMARC's revised IACUC met officially for the first time on May 5, 2015, to review a set of the most time-sensitive research protocols proposed for USMARC investigations and approved all five that were evaluated. In fact, all ARS facilities have reviewed or are reviewing their existing IACUC protocols for conformity to existing policies and will make revisions as appropriate.
- In addition, ARS is working with APHIS to actively review the feasibility of implementing APHIS inspections of ARS research facilities (as outlined by the Action Plan). If the review finds this to be a viable and appropriate course of action, USDA will move to put this proposal into effect. This arrangement would provide APHIS inspections of ARS facilities similar to those provided to other AWA-exempt organizations, such as the National Zoo.
- *Attending veterinarian should not serve as the chair of the USMARC IACUC.* A new panel chair has been appointed. USMARC research physiologist Jeff Vallet, who is not the USMARC attending veterinarian, has assumed the role of Chair of the IACUC.
- *Use of all vertebrate animals at USMARC should be reviewed and approved by the IACUC.* This has been implemented and will continue to be an ongoing practice.

ARS' goal is to continuously improve its management and research practices and has taken immediate actions to address AHWRP recommendations. Of the seven AHWRP recommendations listed above, three were completed in March. An additional two were completed in May. We anticipate the completion of the final recommendation by July 2015.

1.3. ARS Review

The AHWRP will begin its review of ARS animal welfare programs in April 2015. The panel plans to visit three to five ARS locations where animal research is conducted. The AHWRP will prepare a report in October 2015 to the REE Under Secretary summarizing its findings and recommendations. The report will summarize the panel's findings specific to each location visited and generalized findings for ARS agency-wide. The report will identify the panel's conclusions as to whether the care and handling of animals and the capacity of facilities and staff at each location are in compliance with ARS Policies and Procedures (P&Ps) and industry standards, taking into account that ARS has a research mission, not a production mission. In addition, the report will make location-specific and agency-wide recommendations to improve compliance, if necessary, with ARS P&Ps and industry standards and, if appropriate, for changes to ARS P&Ps providing oversight of livestock animal care in ARS' research settings.

APPENDIX B – ANIMAL WELFARE LEADERSHIP COMMITTEE AND TASK FORCE

An Animal Welfare Leadership Committee and an Animal Welfare Task Force lead the ARS animal welfare program. The purpose of the Animal Welfare Leadership Committee is to provide a focused forum for coordinating and collaborating on mechanisms to review and strengthen relevant ARS animal welfare programs and to assist Agency leadership in fulfilling its responsibilities to provide oversight and support of the implementation and effectiveness of the Agency's animal welfare procedures, policies, programs, and initiatives. The Animal Welfare Leadership Committee promotes and encourages the highest level of ethics within the profession of laboratory animal science. The Animal Welfare Leadership Committee provides guidance to the Animal Welfare Task Force and oversees the development and implementation of the roadmap. The Animal Welfare Leadership Committee members include:

- Dr. Steven Kappes, Deputy Administrator, Office of National Programs (Chair)
- Ms. Lisa Baldus, Associate Deputy Administrator, Administrative and Financial Management (AFM) (Alternate)

- Dr. Deborah Brennan, Director, Southeast Area
- Dr. Larry Chandler, Director, Plains Area
- Mr. Nino Fleri, Director, Facilities Division, AFM
- Dr. Andrew Hammond, Director, Pacific West Area
- Mr. Pete Jovanovich, Branch Chief, Safety, Health and Environmental Management Branch, Facilities Division, AFM
- Mr. Joseph Kozlovac, ARS Agency Biosafety Officer
- Dr. Bob Matteri, Director, Midwest Area
- Mr. Joon Park, Deputy Administrator, AFM
- Dr. Dariusz Swietlik, Director, North East Area

The purpose of the Animal Welfare Task Force is to oversee, lead, or participate in the ARS Animal Welfare program inspections, to identify gaps in current ARS animal care and use protocols and procedures, and to develop implementation plans to address identified gaps. The Animal Welfare Task Force members include:

- Dr. Eileen Thacker, DVM, PhD, DACVM, National Program Leader, Food Safety and Animal Health, Office of National Programs, Beltsville, MD
- Ms. Janice Boarman, Program Analyst, Animal Production and Protection, Beltsville, MD
- Dr. Deborah Brennan, DVM, MPA, Director, Southeast Area, Stoneville, MS
- Dr. Donald Knowles, DVM, PhD. DACVP, Research Leader, Animal Disease Research Unit, Pullman, WA
- Mr. Joseph Kozlovac, ARS Agency Biosafety Officer, Beltsville, MD
- Dr. Donald Lay, Jr., PhD, Research Leader, Livestock Behavior Research, West Lafayette, IN
- Dr. Nora Wineland, DVM, MS, DACVPM, Director, APHIS Center for Animal Welfare, Kansas City, MO

APPENDIX C – ANIMAL WELFARE OMBUDSMAN

On January 23, 2015, ARS National Program Leader (NPL) Eileen Thacker was appointed as the first Animal Welfare Ombudsman at ARS. Since 2010, Dr. Thacker has overseen and validated the collection of ARS animal welfare data and ensured that the makeup of the IACUC committees met all requirements of the Animal Welfare Act. Dr. Thacker, a veterinarian with a Ph.D. in pathology, is an NPL for both Food Safety and Animal Health and is Board Certified in Veterinary Microbiology.

The ARS Animal Welfare Ombudsman provides confidential, impartial, and independent assistance to individuals and groups who have complaints or concerns related to animal welfare in ARS animal research facilities. Key operational principles include:

- Confidential – The Animal Welfare Ombudsman maintains the privacy of the identity of individuals or groups as well as the content of their complaints or concerns. The Animal Welfare Ombudsman may contact individuals within ARS whose help is necessary to resolve a complaint or concern.
- Impartial – The Animal Welfare Ombudsman has no personal interest or stake in and incurs no personal gain or loss from the outcome of any complaint or concern process. The Animal Welfare Ombudsman attempts to promote fair processes but does not advocate for individuals or groups on the basis of affiliation or constituency status.
- Independent – The Animal Welfare Ombudsman operates independently of ARS' ordinary line and staff structures. The Animal Welfare Ombudsman exercises total discretion regarding her responsibilities.

The ARS Animal Welfare Ombudsman is impartial and independent of the management structure within ARS. The Animal Welfare Ombudsman reports directly to the ARS Administrator. This reporting structure aims to demonstrate ARS' commitments to animal welfare and establish the credibility of the Animal Welfare Ombudsman.

1.1. Primary Functions

The ARS Animal Welfare Ombudsman does not replace but rather complements and supplements other programs or resources within ARS. The Animal Welfare Ombudsman works in concert with different programs or services in ARS to help with resolution of Animal Welfare complaints or concerns, but does so in a manner that preserves the confidentiality of the individual(s) or group(s) who seek ombudsman services. The Animal Welfare Ombudsman performs a number of functions in carrying out her responsibilities. The primary functions include:

- Provide a safe and confidential forum to service complaints or concerns about animal welfare from internal and external individuals or groups.
- Listen to and help clarify complaints or concerns. Help identify underlying issues and interests. Explore possible options through formal or informal channels.
- Help identify undetected and/or unreported unethical behavior, policy violations, or ineffective animal care and use programs.
- Help employees become empowered and take responsibility for creating humane care and use of animals to support research.
- Provide an early warning diagnosis system that identifies and alerts ARS leaders to any negative trends.
- Provide ARS with an independent and impartial voice, which fosters consistency between ARS' values and actions. Make systemic recommendations for change.
- Collect general data on emerging trends and patterns in ARS' use and care of animals. Provide upward feedback to management about agency trends.

1.2. Communications and Reporting

The Animal Welfare Ombudsman serves as a central point of information and referral resource for Animal Welfare policies, processes, and resources within ARS. The Animal Welfare Ombudsman establishes and monitors an email portal, animalwellbeing@ars.usda.gov, to encourage internal and external communications about ARS animal welfare concerns or complaints.

The Animal Welfare Ombudsman provides reports to the ARS Administrator on an annual basis. Reports should be provided without jeopardizing individuals' confidentiality. The Ombudsman's annual report will include the number of complainants assisted; complainant demographics (e.g., gender, constituent group, college, major or discipline, etc.); problem categories; issues and observations; trends; concerns; and recommendations. In addition to summarizing the results of the year's work, the annual report will alert the ARS leadership to problems and trends and help decision-making within ARS to foster a renewed culture of animal welfare.

APPENDIX D – ANIMAL WELFARE TRAINING PROGRAM

1. Animal Welfare Training

The Animal Welfare Act (AWA) and the Public Health Service (PHS) Policy on Humane Care and Use of Laboratory Animals provide guidance and regulations to ensure that all animals used for research in the United States are treated in a humane manner. It has been the policy of ARS to adhere to and follow all regulations of the AWA and PHS to ensure that the animals used in research by the agency are treated appropriately and humanely. An integral part of both the AWA and the PHS guidelines is a comprehensive animal welfare training program.

2.1. Training Objectives and Scope

The Animal Welfare training program is designed to meet USDA and ARS requirements for basic and specialized training in the humane care and use of animals. Major objectives include:

- Ensuring that research staff members performing experimental manipulation, including anesthesia and surgery, are qualified through training or experience to accomplish such procedures humanely and in a scientifically acceptable fashion.
- Ensuring that individuals who use or provide care for animals are trained and qualified in the appropriate species-specific housing methods, husbandry procedures, and handling techniques.
- Ensuring compliance with any initial and continuing education regarding ARS P&P requirements for care, use, handling, and well-being of animals to support research.

The ARS training program has been designed to meet the training needs of:

- Researchers who use or plan to use animals
- Post-docs

- Technicians
- IACUC members
- Animal care staff
- Animal surgery staff
- Management or administrative staff

For researchers and laboratory staff, training on the safe and humane care for each of the species of animals on which research is conducted would be required, or, if staff already has been trained, documentation would be provided. Training on new procedures and protocols would be required and oversight provided by the IACUC to ensure adequate familiarity with each species and technique. Training and documentation of training would also be required for animal caretakers on all species of animals with which they interact. In addition, all researchers and laboratory personnel would be required to be familiar with the American Veterinary Medical Association (AVMA) Guide on Humane Euthanasia protocols to ensure the appropriate procedures are practiced to euthanize animals (https://www.avma.org).

All employees at ARS locations with animals need to receive training that provides an overview of Animal Care and Use and the AWA within the first 60 days of approval and implementation of this plan or within the first 60 days of employment. Employees of locations co-located with Universities and receiving training associated with the University would be required to provide documentation of all training within the first 60 days of implementation. All training requirements listed would be required to be completed within 12 months of the official announcement of this action plan.

2.2.Training Resources

The animal welfare training program covers general principles of ethical care and use of animals in ARS research as well as specifics on the care and use of particular species. ARS has identified two major animal welfare training resources: The American Association of Laboratory Animal Science (AALAS) learning library and the Collaborative Institutional Training Initiative (CITI) at the University of Miami. These two resources contain a variety of courses designed for laboratory animal professionals at different career levels. A set of animal-specific courses are available that provide information pertinent to specific animals including Amphibians, Cats, Dogs, Ferrets, Fish, Gerbils, Guinea Pigs, Hamsters, Horses, Mice, Non-Human Primates, Rabbits, Rats, Swine, and Zebra-fish. These courses provide an introduction to the regulatory mandates and biological components of individual animals. Additional courses are also available that provide training on the role and responsibilities of ARS management and administrative staff responsible for animal care and use programs.

Both AALAS and CITI training courses are web-based and accessible online at any time and from anywhere. ARS will expand existing arrangements to establish an agency-wide contract to enable all animal research locations to access these training courses. Most of these online courses have test questions to evaluate learning outcomes and ensure that learning objectives are achieved. Additional free animal welfare training courses, webinars, and podcasts are available through University of Newcastle in Australia, Canadian Council on Animal Care, The Canadian Aquaculture Institute, Animal and Plant Health Inspection Service (APHIS), and the National Institutes of Health's Office of Laboratory Animal Welfare. The following table lists Animal Welfare training sources and associated delivery methods.

Training Sources	Delivery Methods
American Association for Laboratory Animal Science (AALAS) learning library https://www.aalaslearninglibrary.org/pages/ Home.aspx	Online with test
The Collaborative Institutional Training Initiative (CITI) at the University of Miami, Animal Care and Use https://www.citiprogram.org/index.cfm?pageID=91	Online with test
University of Newcastle, Animal Welfare and Training Unit https://www.newcastle.edu.au/research-and-innovation/resources/animal-welfare-and-training/about-us	Online
Canadian Council on Animal Care http://www.ccac.ca/en/training/niaut	Online
The Canadian Aquaculture Institute http://www.upei.ca/programsandcourses/canadian-aquaculture-institute	Online
APHIS http://aast.cfsph.iastate.edu/AWIC/awic0020.htm	Online
Education Resources, Office of Laboratory Animal Welfare, NIH http://grants.nih.gov/grants/OLAW/educationalresources.htm#a04052009	Webinars Podcasts

2.3. Training Curriculum

Currently, ARS has many locations that either have animals or have had a recent history of animal research. There is a great diversity by location in the type of research, the animal species involved, and the composition of the

IACUC. The types of research conducted by ARS are variable and may involve biomedical research, animal surgery or challenge of animals with pathogens, as well as non-invasive research to understand production and management strategies. Species involved in ARS research include small rodents, cattle, swine, sheep, poultry, and fish. Therefore, training for each of the locations must be tailored to the type of research and species of animals used to ensure animal welfare and care are specific for each location and research project.

The animal welfare training curriculum consists of basic, elective, and refresher training courses. Basic courses provide a general understanding of Federal policies and regulations governing animal welfare and industry best practices. Elective courses offer animal-specific and specialized courses to learners based on their research activities. Refresher training on animal welfare basics would be required annually for all staff involved in the care and use of animals or oversight of the ARS animal welfare program. Species- or project-specific training will occur prior to work being conducted and refresher/update training as needed due to protocol changes or once every three years or in conjunction with the new program cycle in the appropriate areas for all relevant personnel. Finally, ARS is exploring options with APHIS to jointly develop customized courses on selective topics. Typically, training begins with basic courses, followed by elective courses, and reinforced by refresher courses that ARS staff would complete annually.

Categories	Objectives	Audiences	Courses
Basic	Understand Federal policies and regulations governing animal welfare and animal welfare best practices.	All employees at ARS locations with animals	• Animal Welfare Act Regulations • 8th Edition of the Guide for the Care and Use of Laboratory Animals • Good Laboratory Practice Regulations
Elective	Understand job-specific roles, responsibilities, and best practices.	Scientific staff who uses or plans to use animals in research	• Courses on the species used in research (amphibians, cats, dogs, ferrets, fish, gerbils, guinea pigs, hamsters, mice, rabbits, sheep and goats, swine)

Categories	Objectives	Audiences	Courses
			• Working with the IACUC
		Animal care staff	• Environmental Enrichment for Laboratory Animals • Laboratory Animal Nutrition • Courses on the species for which they provide care (amphibians, cats, dogs, ferrets, fish, gerbils, guinea pigs, hamsters, mice, rabbits, sheep and goats, swine)
		IACUC members	• Essentials for IACUC members (multiple courses including IACUC 101 Series) • Avoiding Financial Conflict of Interest in Federal Research • Common Compliance Issues
		Animal surgery staff	• Training for surgery on the species that is appropriate. • If no training modules are available, training will need to be obtained from personnel trained in performing surgery on the specific species and techniques and approved and documented by the IACUC.
		All employees at ARS	• Complete one refresher basic course annually. • Complete one refresher

Categories	Objectives	Audiences	Courses
		locations with animals	elective course annually.
		Selective ARS staff members	• ARS-specific training courses • ARS and APHIS jointly developed courses

INDEX

E

F

G

Q

R

S

V

W